D0222268

Allyn & Bacon
Casebook Series
Medical Social Work

Edited by

Jerry L. Johnson

Grand Valley State University

George Grant, Jr.

Grand Valley State University

PEARSON

Boston   New York   San Francisco
Mexico City   Montreal   Toronto   London   Madrid   Munich   Paris
Hong Kong   Singapore   Tokyo   Cape Town   Sydney

To all of those who have helped, advised, supported, criticized,
and forgiven. You know who you are.
Jerry L. Johnson

To my wife, Beverly, who inspires and supports me
in all my endeavors. In loving memory of my father and mother,
George and Dorothy Grant.
George Grant, Jr.

Series Editor: *Patricia Quinlin*
Marketing Manager: *Kris Ellis-Levy*
Production Administrator: *Janet Domingo*
Compositor: *Galley Graphics*
Composition Buyer: *Linda Cox*
Manufacturing Buyer: *JoAnne Sweeney*
Cover Coordinator: *Rebecca Krzyzaniak*

For related titles and support materials, visit our online catalog at www.ablongman.com.

Copyright © 2005 Pearson Education, Inc.

All rights reserved. No part of the material protected by this copyright notice may be reproduced or utilized in any form or by any means, electronic or mechanical, including photocopying, recording, or by any information storage and retrieval system, without written permission from the copyright owner.

To obtain permission(s) to use material from this work, please submit a written request to Allyn and Bacon, Permissions Department, 75 Arlington Street, Boston, MA 02116 or fax your request to 617-848-7320.

Library of Congress Cataloging-in-Publication Data

Allyn & Bacon casebook series for medical social work / edited by Jerry L. Johnson,
George Grant, Jr.—1st ed.
   p. cm.
   Includes bibliographical references.
   ISBN 0-205-38948-1 (pbk.)
   1. Medical social work—Case studies.   2. Social case work.   I. Title: Allyn and Bacon
casebook series for medical social work.   II. Title: Casebook series for medical social work.
III. Johnson, Jerry L.   IV. Grant, George, Jr.
HV875. A37 2005
362.1'0425—dc22

                                            2004056832

Printed in the United States of America

10 9 8 7 6 5 4 3   09 08 07

Contents

iii

Preface

This text offers students the chance to study the work of experienced social workers practicing in various health and medical practice settings. As graduate and undergraduate social work educators, we (the editors) have struggled to find quality practice materials that translate well into a classroom setting. Over the years, we have used case materials from our practice careers, professionally produced audiovisuals, and tried other casebooks. While each had its advantages, we could not find a vehicle that allowed students to study the work of experienced practitioners that took students beyond the belief that practice is a technical endeavor that involves finding "correct" interventions to solve client problems.

We want our students to study and analyze how experienced practitioners think about practice and how they struggle to resolve ethical dilemmas and make treatment decisions that meet the needs of their clientele. We want students to review and challenge the work of others in a way that allows them to understand what comprises important practice decisions with real clients in real practice settings. That is, we want classroom materials that allow students entry into the minds of experienced practitioners.

Goals of the Casebook

This Casebook focuses on practice in medical social work and with clients in a variety of settings and from diverse backgrounds. Our goal is to provide students with an experience that:

1. Provides personal and intimate glimpses into the thinking and actions of experienced practitioners as they work with clients. In each case, students may demonstrate their understanding of the cases and how and/or why the authors approached their case in the manner presented.

2. Provides a vehicle to evaluate the process, ideas, and methods used by the authors. We also wanted to provide students a chance to present their ideas about how they would have worked differently with the same case.
3. Affords students the opportunity to use evidence-based practice findings (Gibbs, 2003; Cournoyer, 2004) as part of the case review and planning process. We challenge students to base practice judgments and case planning exercises on current practice evidence available through library and/or electronic searches, and practice wisdom gained through consultation and personal experience when the evidence is conflicted or lacking.

To meet our goals, the cases we included in this text focus on the practice process, specifically client engagement, assessment, and the resultant clinical process, including the inevitable ethical dilemmas that consistently arise in daily practice. We aim to demonstrate the technical and artistic elements involved in developing and managing the various simultaneous processes involved in practice. While we recognize the difficulty of presenting process information (circular) in a linear medium (book), we have tried to do the best job possible toward this end.

To achieve our goals, we include four in-depth case studies in this text. Authors guide students through the complete practice process, from initial contact to client termination and practice evaluation. Focusing heavily on multi-systemic client life history (see Chapter 1), students get a detailed look into the life history and presentation of the client. Then, we challenge students to "finish the case" by using client information and classroom learning to develop a written narrative assessment, diagnostic statement, treatment and intervention plan, termination and follow-up plan, and a plan to evaluate practice. We have used these cases as in-class exercises, the basis for semester-long term papers, and as comprehensive final examinations that integrate multifaceted student learning in practice courses across the curriculum.

Rationale

As former practitioners, we chose the cases carefully. Therefore, the cases in this text focus on the process (thinking, planning, and decision-making) of social work practice and not necessarily on techniques or outcome. Do not be fooled by this statement. Obviously, we believe in successful client outcome based, at least in part, on the use of evidence-based practice methods and current research findings. As important as this is, it is not our focus here with good reason. Our experience suggests that instructive process occurs in cases that have successful and unsuccessful outcome. In fact, we often learned more from unsuccessful cases than successful cases. We learned the most when events did not play out as planned. While some of the cases terminated successfully, others did not. This is not a commentary on the author or the author's skill level. Everyone has cases (sometimes too many) that do not turn out as planned. We chose cases based on one simple criterion: did it provide the best possible hope for practice education? We asked authors to teach practice by considering cases that were interesting and difficult, regardless of outcome. We did not want the Casebook to become simply a vehicle to promote practice brilliance.

Mostly, we wanted this text to differ from other casebooks, because we were unsatisfied with casebooks as teaching tools. As part of the process of planning our Casebooks, we reviewed other casebooks and discussed with our graduate and undergraduate students approaches that best facilitated learning in the classroom. We discovered that many students were also dissatisfied with a casebook approach to education, for a variety of reasons. Below, we briefly address what our students told us about casebooks in general.

1. *Linear presentation.* One of the most significant problems involves case presentation. Generally, this involves two issues: linearity and brevity. Most written case studies give students the impression that practice actually proceeds smoothly, orderly, and in a sequential manner. These cases often leave students believing or expecting that clinical decisions are made beforehand and that practice normally proceeds as planned. In other words, students often enter the field believing that casework follows an "*A, leads to B, leads to C, leads to clients living happily ever after*" approach.

Experienced practitioners know better. In over 40 years of combined social work practice in a variety of settings, we have learned often the "hard way" that the opposite is true. We rarely, if ever, had a case proceed sequentially, whether our client is an individual, couple, family, group, community, or classroom. That is, the process of engagement (including cultural competence), assessment, treatment planning, intervention, and follow-up occur in a circular manner, rooted in the client's social, physical, and cultural context, and includes consideration of the practitioner, his or her organization, and the laws and policies that affect and/or determine the boundaries of social work practice and treatment funding.

Practice evolves in discontinuous cycles over time, including time-limited treatments mandated by the managed care system. Therefore, real-life clinical practice just as in all developing human relationships seems to consistently require stops and starts, take wrong turns, and even, in some cases, require "do-overs." While the goal of competent practice is to facilitate an orderly helping process that includes planned change (Timberlake, Farber, & Sabatino, 2002), practice, as an orderly process, is more often a goal (or a myth) than planned certainty. Given the linearity of case presentations discussed above, readers are often left without an appreciation or understanding of practice as process.

Additionally, many of the case presentation texts we reviewed provided "hard" client data and asked students to develop treatment plans based on this data. Yet, as any experienced practitioner knows, the difficulty in practice occurs during engagement and data collection. The usual case approach often overlooks this important element of practice. While a book format limits process writing, we believe that the case format we devised here brings students closer to the "real thing."

2. *Little focus on client engagement.*   As we like to remind students, there are two words in the title of our profession: social and work. In order for the "work" to be successful, students must learn to master the "social," primarily client engagement and relationship building. Social work practice is relationship based (Saleebey, 2002) and, from our perspective, relies more on the processes involved in relationship building and client engagement than technical intervention skills (Johnson, 2004). Successful practice is often rooted more in the ability of practitioners to develop open and trusting relationships with client(s) than on their ability to employ specific methods of intervention (Johnson, 2004).

Yet, this critically important element of practice often goes understated or ignored. Some texts even assume that engagement skills somehow exist before learning about practice. We find this true in casebooks and primary practice texts as well. When it is discussed, engagement and relationship building is presented as a technical process that also proceeds in linear fashion. Our experience with students, employees, and practitioner/trainees over the last two decades suggests that it is wrong to assume that students and/or practitioners have competent engagement or relationship building skills. From our perspective, developing a professional relationship that involves trust and openness, where clients feel safe to dialogue about the most intimate and sometimes embarrassing events in their lives, is the primary responsibility of the practitioner, and often spells the difference between positive and negative client outcome (Johnson, 2004; Miller & Rollnick, 2002; Harper & Lantz, 1996). Hence, each case presentation tries to provide a sense of this difficult and often elusive process and some of the ways that the authors overcame challenges to the culturally competent client engagement process.

Target Audience

Our target audience for this text, and the others in the series, are advanced undergraduate as well as foundation and advanced graduate students in social work and other helping disciplines. We have tested our approach with students at several different points in their education. We find that the casebooks can be used as:

- An adjunct learning tool for undergraduates preparing for or already involved in their field practicum.
- Practice education and training for foundation-level graduate students in practice theory and/or methods courses.
- An adjunct learning tool for second-year graduate students in field practicum.

- An adjunct learning tool for undergraduate and/or graduate students in any practice courses pertaining to specific populations.

While we are social work educators, we believe the casebooks will be useful in social work and other disciplines in the human services, including counseling psychology, counseling, mental health, psychology, and specialty disciplines such as marriage and family therapy, substance abuse, and mental health degree or certificate programs. Any educational or training program designed to prepare students to work with clients in a helping capacity may find the casebooks useful as a learning tool.

Structure of Cases

We organized the case studies to maximize critical thinking, the use of professional literature, evidenced-based practice knowledge, and classroom discussion in the learning process. At various points throughout each case, we comment on issues and/or dilemmas highlighted by the case. Our comments always end with a series of questions designed to focus student learning by calling on their ability to find and evaluate evidence from the professional literature and through classroom discussion. We ask students to collect evidence on different sides of an issue, evaluate that evidence, and develop a professional position that they can defend in writing and/or discussion with other students in the classroom or seminar setting.

We hope that you find the cases and our format as instructive and helpful in your courses as we have in ours. We have field-tested our format in courses at our university, finding that students respond well to the length, depth, and rigor of the case presentations. Universally, students report that the case materials were an important part of their overall learning process.

Organization of the Text

We organized this text to maximize its utility in any course. Chapter 1 provides an overview of the Advanced Multi-Systemic (AMS) practice approach. We provide this as one potential organizing tool for students to use while reading and evaluating the subsequent cases. This chapter offers students an organized and systematic framework to use when analyzing cases and/or formulating narrative assessments, treatment, and intervention plans. Our intent is to provide a helpful tool, not make a political statement about the efficacy or popularity of one practice framework versus others. In fact, we invite faculty and students to apply whatever practice framework they wish when working the cases.

In Chapter 2, author *Joan M. Borst, MSW, CSW* presents her work with **Bob and Phil,** a gay couple suffering through multiple diagnoses of HIV/AIDS and the problems associated with this life-changing medical condition. This case is an excellent example of the multiple problems that occur when one or both partners discover they have HIV/AIDS. Borst traces her work with Bob and Phil from the moments immediately following initial diagnosis to the case's completion several years hence. She demonstrates the involvement of multi-systemic factors in her work with this couple.

In Chapter 3, *Rose Malinowski, DrPH, LCSW* presents a case involving a pregnant teenager and her mother in a hospital social work setting. In a case entitled **Stephanie and Rose Doer,** Dr. Malinowski demonstrates the problems that occur when a young woman gives birth to a developmentally disabled infant after concealing her pregnancy from her mother. This case also demonstrates the impact of the birth on the family and a hospital's response to this crisis.

In Chapter 4, *Joan M. Borst, MSW, CSW* offers a second case involving a homeless 19-year-old woman needing healthcare services. In a case entitled **Annie,** Borst takes readers through a difficult case that involves the many issues, problems, and systemic barriers that face homeless women of color trying to survive living on the streets in a big city.

The final chapter, **Mrs. Smith and Her Family,** presents the work of *Doreen R. McGrath, MSW, CSW* with the extended families of an elderly woman on life support. This case focuses on the problems facing families when life and death decisions are imminent, and the hospital social worker's role as a helper. It also demonstrates the social worker's need for multiple systems involvement as McGrath navigates the family through the legal process associated with appointing a temporary guardian.

Acknowledgments

We would like to thank the contributors to this text, Joan M. Borst, Rose Malinowski, and Doreen R. McGrath, for their willingness to allow their work to be challenged and discussed in a public venue. We would also like to thank Patricia Quinlin and her people at Allyn and Bacon for their faith in the Casebook Series and in our ability to manage fourteen manuscripts at once. Additionally, we have to thank all of our students and student assistants that served as "guinea pigs" for our case studies. Their willingness to provide honest feedback contributes mightily to this series.

Jerry L. Johnson—I want to thank my wife, Cheryl, for her support and willingness to give me the time and encouragement to write and edit. I also owe a debt of gratitude to my dear friend Hope, for being there when I need you the most.

George Grant, Jr.—I want to thank Dean Rodney Mulder and Dr. Elaine Schott for their insight, encouragement, and support during this process. I also thank Dr. Julius Franks and Professor Daniel Groce for their intellectual discourse and unwavering support.

Contributors

The Editors

Jerry L. Johnson, Ph.D., MSW is an Associate Professor in the School of Social Work at Grand Valley State University in Grand Rapids, Michigan. He received his MSW from Grand Valley State University and his Ph.D. in sociology from Western Michigan University. Johnson has been in social work for more than 20 years as a practitioner, supervisor, administrator, consultant, teacher, and trainer. He was the recipient of two Fulbright Scholarship awards to Albania in 1998–99 and 2000–01. In addition to teaching and writing, Johnson serves in various consulting capacities in countries such as Albania and Armenia. He is the author of two previous books, *Crossing Borders—Confronting History: Intercultural Adjustment in a Post-Cold War World* (2000, Rowan and Littlefield) and *Fundamentals of Substance Abuse Practice* (2004, Wadsworth Brooks/Cole).

George Grant, Jr., Ph.D., MSW is an Associate Professor in the School of Social Work at Grand Valley State University in Grand Rapids, Michigan. Grant, Jr., also serves as the Director of Grand Valley State University's MSW Program. He received his MSW from Grand Valley State University and Ph.D. in sociology from Western Michigan University. Grant, Jr., has a long and distinguished career as practitioner, administrator, consultant, teacher, and trainer in social work, primarily in fields dedicated to Child Welfare.

Contributors

Joan M. Borst, MSW, CSW is Assistant Professor of Social Work and the BSW Program Director at Grand Valley State University in Grand Rapids, Michigan. She has taught in various capacities for 10 years. Ms. Borst had practiced social work health care with people who are homeless and people living with chronic illnesses, such as HIV/AIDS, cancers, and mental illness. She has worked in clinics, outpatient, and inpatient settings. Borst is currently a Ph.D. candidate in Social Work at Michigan State University.

Rose Malinowski, DrPH, LCSW is Director of Field Education in the Social Work Department at Trinity Christian College in Palos Heights, Illinois. She received her MSW degree from Loyola University in Chicago and her Doctorate in Public Health at the University of Illinois at Chicago.

Doreen R. McGrath, MSW, CSW received her B.S. degree in Family Studies from Central Michigan University. She was awarded her MSW degree from Grand Valley State University in 1998. She has practiced hospital social work for Spectrum Health in Grand Rapids, Michigan, since 1998. Her other professional interest is long-term health care. She served her field practicum at the Christian Rest Home, also in Grand Rapids, Michigan.

Bibliography _____

Cournoyer, B. R. (2004). *The evidence-based social work skills book.* Boston: Allyn and Bacon.

Gibbs, L. E. (2003). *Evidence-based practice for the helping professions: A practical guide with integrated multimedia.* Pacific Grove, CA: Brooks/Cole.

Harper, K. V., & Lantz, J. (1996). *Cross-cultural practice: Social work practice with diverse populations.* Chicago: Lyceum Books.

Johnson, J. L. (2004). *Fundamentals of substance abuse practice.* Pacific Grove, CA: Brooks/Cole.

Miller, W. R., & Rollnick, S. (2002). *Motivational interviewing: Preparing people to change addictive behavior* (2nd ed.). New York: Guilford Press.

Saleebey, D. (2002). *The strengths perspective in social work practice* (3rd ed.). Boston: Allyn and Bacon.

Timberlake, E. M., Farber, M. Z., & Sabatino, C. A. (2002). *The general method of social work practice: McMahon's generalist perspective* (4th ed.). Boston: Allyn and Bacon.

1

A Multi-Systemic Approach to Practice

Jerry L. Johnson & George Grant, Jr.

This is a practice-oriented text, designed to build practice skills with individuals, families, and groups. We intend to provide you the opportunity to study the process involved in treating real cases from the caseloads of experienced practitioners. Unlike other casebooks, we include fewer cases, but provide substantially more detail in hopes of providing a realistic look into the thinking, planning, and approach of the practitioners/authors. We challenge you to study the authors' thinking and methods to understand their approach and then use critical thinking skills and the knowledge you have gained in your education and practice to propose alternative ways of treating the same clients. In other words, what would your course of action be if you were the primary practitioner responsible for these cases? Our hope is that this text provides a worthwhile and rigorous experience studying real cases as they progressed in practice.

Before proceeding to the cases, we include this chapter as an introduction to the Advanced Multi-Systemic (AMS) practice perspective. We decided to present this introduction with two primary goals in mind. First, we want you to use the information contained in this chapter to help assess and analyze the cases in this text. You will have the opportunity to complete a multi-systemic assessment, diagnoses, treatment, and intervention plan for each case. This chapter will provide the theoretical and practical basis for this exercise. Second, we hope you find that AMS makes conceptualizing cases clearer in your practice environment. We do not suggest that AMS is the only way, or even the best way for every practitioner to conceptualize cases. We simply know, through experience, that AMS is an effective way to think about practice with client-systems of all sizes and configurations. While there are many approaches to practice, AMS offers an effective way to place clinical decisions in the context of client lives and experiences, making engagement and treatment productive for clients and practitioners.

Advanced Multi-Systemic (AMS) Practice

Sociological Roots

> Whether the point of interest is a great power state or a minor literary mood, a family, a prison, and a creed—these are the kinds of questions the best social analysts have asked. They are the intellectual pivots of classic studies of (person) in society—and they are the questions inevitably raised by any mind possessing the sociological imagination. For that imagination is the capacity to shift from one perspective to another—from the political to the psychological; from examination of a single family to comparative assessment of the national budgets of the world; from the theological school to the military establishment; from considerations of an oil industry to studies of contemporary poetry. It is the capacity to range from the most impersonal and remote transformations to the most intimate features of the human self—and see the relations between the two. Back of its use is always the urge to know the social and historical meaning of the individual in the society and in the period in which he (or she) has his quality and his (or her) being. (Mills, 1959, p. 7; parentheses added)

Above, sociologist C. Wright Mills provided a seminal description of the sociological imagination. As it turns out, Mills's sociological imagination is also an apt description of AMS. Mills believed that linking people's "private troubles" to "public issues" (p. 2) was the most effective way to understand people and their issues, by placing them in historical context. It forces investigators to contextualize individuals and families in the framework of the larger social, political, economic, and historical environments in which they live. Ironically, this is also the goal of social work practice (Germain & Gitterman, 1996; Longres, 2000). Going further, Mills (1959) stated:

> We have come to know that every individual lives, from one generation to the next, in some society; that he (or she) lives out a biography, and that he (or she) lives it out within some historical sequence. By the fact of his (or her) living he (or she) contributes, however minutely, to the shaping of this society and to the course of its history, even as he (or she) is made by society and by its historical push and shove. (p. 6)

Again, Mills was not speaking as a social worker. He was an influential sociologist, speaking about a method of social research. In *The Sociological Imagination,* Mills (1959) proposed this as a method to understand the links between people, their daily lives, and their multi-systemic environment. Yet, while laying the theoretical groundwork for social research, Mills also provided the theoretical foundation for an effective approach to social work practice. We find four relevant points in *The Sociological Imagination* that translate directly to social work practice.

1. It is crucial to recognize the relationships between people's personal issues and strengths (private troubles) and the issues (political, economic, social, historical, and legal) and strengths of the multi-systemic environment (public issues) in which people live daily and across their life span. A multi-systemic understanding includes recognizing and integrating issues and strengths at the micro (individual, family, extended kin, etc.), mezzo (local community), and macro (state, region, national, and international policy, laws, political, economic, and social) levels during client engagement, assessment, treatment, follow-up, and evaluation of practice.

2. This depth of understanding (by social workers and, especially, clients) can lead to change in people's lives. We speak here about second-order change, or, significant change that makes a long-term difference in people's lives; change that helps people view themselves differently in relationship to their world. This level of change becomes possible when people make multi-systemic links in a way that makes sense to them (Freire, 1993). In other words, clients become "empowered" to change when they understand their life in the context of their world and realize that they have previously unforeseen or unimagined choices in how they live, think, believe, and act.

3. Any assessment and/or clinical diagnoses that exclude multi-systemic links do not provide a holistic picture of people's lives, their troubles, and/or strengths. In sociology, this leads to a reductionist view of people and society, while in social work it reduces the likelihood that services will be provided (or received by clients) in a way that addresses client problems and utilizes client strengths in a meaningful way. The opportunity for change is reduced whenever client life history is overlooked because it does not fit, or is not called for, in a practitioner's preferred method of helping, or because of shortcuts many people believe are needed in a managed care environment. One cannot learn too much about their clients, their lives, and their attitudes, beliefs, and values as it relates to the private troubles presented in treatment.

4. Inherent in AMS and foundational to achieving all that was discussed above relies on practitioners being able to rapidly develop rapport with clients that leads to engagement in treatment. In this text, client engagement

> . . . occurs when you develop, in collaboration with clients, a trusting and open professional relationship that promotes hope and presents viable prospects for change. Successful engagement occurs when you create a social context in which vulnerable people (who often hold jaded attitudes toward helping professionals) can share their innermost feelings, as well as their most embarrassing and shameful behavior with you, a total stranger. (Johnson, 2004, p. 93; emphasis in original)

AMS Overview

First, we should define two important terms that comprise AMS. Understanding these terms is important, because they provide the foundation for understanding the language and concepts used throughout the remainder of this chapter.

1. Advanced. According to Derezotes (2000), "the most advanced theory is also the most inclusive" (p. viii). AMS is advanced because it is inclusive. It requires responsible practitioners, in positions of responsibility (perhaps as solo practitioners), to acquire a depth of knowledge, skills, and self-awareness that allows for an inclusive application of knowledge acquired in the areas of human behavior in the social environment, social welfare policy, social research and practice evaluation, and multiple practice methods and approaches in service of clients and client systems of various sizes, types, and configurations.

AMS practitioners are expected to have the most inclusive preparation possible, "both the broad generalist base of knowledge, skills, and values and an in-depth proficiency in practice . . . with selected social work methods and populations" (Derezotes, 2000, p. xii). Hence, advanced practitioners are well trained and, with in-depth knowledge, are often in positions of being responsible for clients as primary practitioners. They are afforded the responsibility for engaging, assessing, intervening, and evaluating practice, ensuring that clients are ethically treated in a way that is culturally competent and respectful of their client's worldview. In other words, AMS practitioners develop the knowledge, skills, and values needed to be leaders in their organizations, communities, the social work profession, and especially in the treatment of their clients. The remainder of this chapter explains why AMS is an advanced approach to practice.

2. Multi-systemic. From the earliest moments in their education, social workers learn a systems perspective that emphasizes the connectedness between people and their problems to the complex interrelationships that exist in their client's world (Timberlake, Farber, & Sabatino, 2002). To explain these connections, systems theory emphasizes three important concepts: wholeness, relationships, and homeostasis. Wholeness refers to the notion that the various parts or elements (subsystem) of a system interact to form a whole that best describes the system in question. This concept asserts that no system can be understood or explained unless the connectedness of the subsystems to the whole are understood or explained. In other words, the whole is greater than the sum of its parts. Moreover, systems theory also posits that change in one subsystem will affect change in the system as a whole.

In terms of systems theory, relationship refers to the patterns of interaction and overall structures that exist within and between subsystems. The nature of these relationships is more important than the system itself. That is, when trying to understand or explain a system (individual, family, or organization, etc.), how subsystems connect through relationships, the characteristics of the relationships between subsystems, and how the subsystems interact provide clues to understanding the system as a whole. Hence, the application of systems theory is primarily based on understanding relationships. As someone once said about systems theory, in systems problems occur between people and subsystems (relationships), not "in" them. People's internal problems relate to the nature of the relationships in the systems where they live and interact.

Homeostasis refers to the notion that most living systems work to maintain and preserve the existing system, or the status quo. For example, family members often assume roles that serve to protect and maintain family stability, often at the expense of "needed" change. The same can be said for organizations or groups. The natural tendency toward homeostasis in systems represents what we call the "dilemma of change" (Johnson, 2004). This can best be described as the apparent conflict, or what appears to be client resistance or lack of motivation, that often occurs when clients approach moments of significant change. Systems of all types and configurations struggle with the dilemma of change: should they change to the unknown or remain the same, even if the status quo is unhealthy or unproductive? Put differently, systems strive for stability, even at the expense of health and well-being of individual members and/or the system itself.

What do we mean then, by the term *multi-systemic*? Clients (individuals, families, etc.) are systems that interact with a number of different systems simultaneously. These systems exist and interact at multiple levels, ranging from the micro level (individual and families), the mezzo level (local community, institutions, organizations, the practitioner and their agency, etc.), to the macro level (culture, laws and policy, politics, oppression and discrimination, international events, etc.). How these various systems come together, interact, and adapt, along with the relationships that exist within and between each system work together to comprise the "whole" that is the client, or client-system. In practice, the client (individual, couple, family, etc.) is not the "system," but one of many interacting subsystems in a maze of other subsystems constantly interacting to create the system—the client plus elements from multiple subsystems at each level. It would be a mistake to view the client as the whole system. They are but one facet of a multidimensional and multi-level system comprised of the client and various other subsystems at the micro, mezzo, and macro levels.

Therefore, the term *multi-systemic* refers to the nature of a system comprised of the various multi-level subsystems described above. A multi-systemic perspective recognizes that clients are *one part or subsystem* in relationship with other subsystemic influences occurring on different levels. This level of understanding—the system as the whole produced through multi-systemic subsystem interactions—is the main unit of investigation for practice. As stated above, it is narrow to consider the client as a functioning independent system with peripheral involvement with other systems existing outside of their intimate world. These issues and relationships work together to help shape and mold the client who in turn, shapes and molds his or her relationship to the other subsystems. Yet, the person-of-the-client is but one part of the system in question during practice.

AMS provides an organized framework for gathering, conceptualizing, and analyzing multi-systemic client data and for proceeding with the helping process. It defines the difference between social work and other disciplines in the helping professions at the level of theory and practice. How, you ask? Unlike other professional disciplines that tend to focus on one or a few domains (i.e., psychology, medicine, etc.), AMS provides a comprehensive and holistic "picture" of clients or client-systems in the context of their environment by considering information about multiple personal and systemic domains simultaneously.

Resting on the generalist foundation taught in all Council on Social Work Education (CSWE) accredited undergraduate and foundation-level graduate programs, AMS requires practitioners to contextualize client issues in the context of the multiple interactions that occur between the client/client-system and the social, economic, legal, political, and physical environment in which the client lives. It is a unifying perspective based in the client's life, history, and culture that guides the process of collecting and analyzing client life information and intervening to promote personal choice through a comprehensive, multi-systemic framework. Beginning with culturally competent client engagement, a comprehensive multi-systemic assessment points toward a holistically based treatment plan that requires practitioners to select and utilize appropriate practice theories, models, and methods—or combinations thereof—that best fit the client's unique circumstances and needs.

AMS is not a practice theory, model, or method itself. It is a perspective or framework for conceptualizing client-systems. It relies on the practitioner's ability to use a variety of theories, models, and methods, and to incorporate knowledge from human behavior, social policy, research/evaluation, and practice into his or her routine approach with clients. For example, an AMS practitioner will have the skills to apply different approaches to individual treatment (client-centered, cognitive-behavioral, etc.), family treatment (structural, narrative, Bowenian, etc.), work with couples, in groups, arrange for specialized care if needed, and as an advocate on behalf of their client. It may also require practitioners to treat clients in a multimodal approach (i.e., individual and group treatments simultaneously).

Practitioners not only must know how to apply different approaches but also how to determine, primarily through the early engagement and assessment process, which theory, model, or approach (direct or indirect, for example) would work best for a particular client. Hence, successful practice using AMS relies heavily on the practitioner's ability to competently engage and multi-systemically assess client problems and strengths. Practitioners must simultaneously develop a sense of their client's personal interaction and relationship style—especially related to how they relate to authority figures—when determining which approach would best suit the client. For example, a reserved, quiet, or thoughtful client or someone who lacks assertiveness may not be well served by a directive, confrontational approach, regardless of the practitioner's preference. Moreover, AMS practitioners rely on professional practice research and outcome studies to help determine which approach or intervention package might work best for particular clients and/or client-systems. AMS expects practitioners to know how to find and evaluate practice research in their practice areas or specialties.

Elements of the Advanced Multi-Systemic Approach to Social Work Practice

The advanced multi-systemic approach entails the following seven distinct, yet integrated elements of theory and practice. Each is explained below.

Ecological Systems Perspective

One important sub-category of systems therapy for social work is the ecological systems perspective. This perspective combines important concepts from the science of ecology and general systems theory into a way of viewing client problems and strengths in social work practice. In recent years, it has become the prevailing perspective for social work practice (Miley, O'Melia, & DuBois, 2004). The ecological systems perspective—sometimes referred to as the ecosystems perspective—is a useful metaphor for guiding social workers as they think about cases (Germain & Gitterman, 1980).

Ecology focuses on how subsystems work together and adapt. In ecology, adaptation is "a dynamic process between people and their environments as people grow, achieve competence, and make contributions to others" (Greif, 1986, p. 225). Insight from ecology leads to an analysis of how people fit within their environment and what adaptations are made in the fit between people and their environments. Problems develop as a function of inadequate or improper adaptation or fit between people and their environments.

General systems theory focuses on how human systems interact. It focuses specifically on how people grow, survive, change, and achieve stability or instability in the complex world of multiple systemic interactions (Miley, O'Melia, & DuBois, 2004). General systems theory has contributed significantly to the growth of the family therapy field and to how social workers understand their clients.

Together, ecology and general systems theory evolved into what social workers know as the ecological systems perspective. The ecological systems perspective provides a systemic framework for understanding the many ways that persons and environments interact. Accordingly, individuals and their individual circumstances can be understood in the context of these interactions. The ecological systems perspective provides an important part of the foundation for AMS. Miley, O'Melia, and DuBois (2004) provide an excellent summary of the ecological systems perspective. They suggest that it

1. Presents a dynamic view of human beings as system interactions in context.
2. Emphasizes the significance of human system interactions.
3. Traces how human behavior and interaction develop over time in response to internal and external forces.
4. Describes current behavior as an adaptive fit of "persons in situations."
5. Conceptualizes all interaction as adaptive or logical in context.
6. Reveals multiple options for change within persons, their social groups, and in their social and physical environments (p. 33).

Social Constructionism

To maintain AMS as an inclusive practice approach, we need to build on the ecological systems perspective by including ideas derived from social constructionism. Social constructionism builds on the ecological systems perspective by introducing ideas about how people define themselves and their environment. Social constructionism also, by definition, introduces the role of culture in the meaning people give to themselves and other systems in their multi-systemic environments. The ecological systems perspective discusses relationships at the systemic level. Social constructionism introduces meaning and value into the equation, allowing for a deeper understanding and appreciation of the nature of multi-systemic relationships and adaptations.

Usually, people assume that reality is something "out there" that hits them in the face, something that independently exists, and people must learn to "deal with it." Social constructionism posits something different. Evolving as a critique of the "one reality" belief system, social constructionism points out that the world is comprised of multiple realities. People define their own reality and then live within those definitions. Accordingly, the definition of reality will be different for everyone. Hence, social constructionism deals primarily with meaning, or the systemic processes by which people come to define themselves in their social world. As sociologist W. I. Thomas said, in what has become known as the Thomas Theorem, "If people define situations as real, they are real in their consequences."

For example, some people believe that they can influence the way computerized slot machines pay out winnings by the way they sit, the feeling they get from the machine as they look at it in the casino, by the clothes they are wearing, or by how they trigger the machine, either by pushing the button or pulling the handle. Likewise, many athletes believe that a particular article of clothing, a routine for getting dressed, and/or a certain pregame meal dictates the quality of their athletic prowess that day.

Illogical to most people, the belief that they can influence a computerized machine, that the machine emits feelings, or that an article of clothing dictates athletic prowess is real to some people. For these people, their beliefs influence the way they live. Perhaps you have ideas or "superstitions" that you believe influence how your life goes on a particular day. This is a common occurrence. These people are not necessarily out of touch with objective reality. While people may know, at some level, that slot machines pay according to preset, computerized odds or that athletic prowess has nothing to do with dressing routines, the belief systems continue. What dictates the behavior and beliefs discussed above or in daily "superstitutions" have nothing to do with objective reality and everything to do with people's subjective reality. Subjective reality—or a person's learned definition of the situation—overrides objectivity and helps determine how people behave and/or what they believe.

While these examples may be simplistic, according to social constructionism, the same processes influence everyone—always. In practice, understanding that people's behavior does not depend on the objective existence of something, but on their subjective interpretation of it, is crucial to effective application of AMS. This knowledge is most helpful during client engagement. If practitioners remember that practice is about understanding people's perceptions and not objective reality, they reduce the likelihood that clients will feel misunderstood, there will be fewer disagreements, and it becomes easier to avoid the trap of defining normal behavior as client resistance or a diagnosable mental disorder. This perspective contributes to a professional relationship based in the client's life and belief systems, is consistent with his or her worldview, and one that is culturally appropriate for the client. Being mindful that the definitions people learn from their culture underlies not only what they do but also what they perceive, feel, and think places practitioners on the correct path to "start where the client is." Social constructionism emphasizes the cultural uniqueness of each client and/or client-system and the need to understand each client and/or client-system in her own context and belief systems, not the practitioner's context or belief systems.

Social constructionism also posits that different people attribute different meaning to the same events, because the interactional contexts and the way individuals interpret these contexts are different for everyone, even within the same family or community. One cannot assume that people raised in the same family will define their social world similarly. Individuals, in the context of their environments, derive meaning through a complex process of individual interpretation. This is how siblings from the same family can be so different, almost as if they did not grow up in the same family. For example, the sound of gunfire in the middle of the night may be frightening or normal, depending upon where a person resides and what is routine and accepted in his specific environment. Moreover, simply because some members of a family or community understand nightly gunfire as normal does not mean that others in the same family or community will feel the same.

Additionally, social constructionism examines how people construct meaning with language and established or evolving cultural beliefs. For example, alcohol consumption is defined as problematic depending upon how the concept of "alcohol problem" is socially constructed in specific environments. Clients from so-called drinking cultures may define drinking six alcoholic drinks daily as normal, while someone from a different cultural background may see this level of consumption as problematic. One of the authors worked in Russia and found an issue that demonstrates this point explicitly. Colleagues in Russia stated rather emphatically that consuming one "bottle" (approximately a U.S. pint) of vodka per day was acceptable and normal. People that consume more than one bottle per day were defined as having a drinking problem. The same level of consumption in the United States would be considered by most as clear evidence of problem drinking.

Biopsychosocial Perspective

Alone, the ecological systems perspective, even with the addition of social constructionism, does not provide the basis for the holistic understanding required by AMS. While it provides a multi-systemic lens, the ecological systems perspective focuses mostly on externals. That is, how people interact and adapt to their environments and how environments interact and adapt to people. Yet, much of what practitioners consider "clinical" focuses on "internals" or human psychological and emotional functioning. Therefore, the ecological systems perspective provides only one part of the holistic picture required by the advanced multi-systemic approach. By adding the biopsychosocial perspective, practitioners can consider the internal workings of human beings to help explain how external and internal subsystems interact.

What is the biopsychosocial perspective? It is a theoretical perspective that considers how human biological, psychological, and social-functioning subsystems interact to account for how people live in their environment. Similar to social systems, human beings are also multidimensional systems comprised of multiple subsystems constantly interacting in their environment, the human body. The biopsychosocial perspective applies multi-systemic thinking to individual human beings.

Several elements comprise the biopsychosocial perspective. Longres (2000) identifies two dimensions of individual functioning, the biophysical and the psychological; subdividing the psychological into three subdimensions: the cognitive, affective, and behavioral. Elsewhere, we added the spiritual/existential dimension to this conception (Johnson, 2004). Understanding how the biological, psychological, spiritual and existential, and social subsystems interact is instrumental in developing an appreciation of how individuals influence and are influenced by their social systemic environments. Realizing that each of these dimensions interacts with external social and environmental systems allow practitioners to enlarge their frame of reference, leading to a more holistic multi-systemic view of clients and client-systems.

Strengths/Empowerment Perspective

Over the last few years, the strengths perspective has emerged as an important part of social work theory and practice. The strengths perspective represents a significant change in how social workers conceptualize clients and client-systems. According to Saleebey (2002), it is "a versatile practice approach, relying heavily on ingenuity and creativity. . . . Rather than focusing on problems, your eye turns toward possibility" (p. 1). Strengths-based practitioners believe in the power of possibility and hope in helping people overcome problems by focusing on, locating, and supporting existing personal or systemic strengths and resiliencies. The strengths perspective is based on the belief that people, regardless of the severity of their problems, have the capabilities and resources to play an active role in helping solve their own problems. The practitioner's role is to engage clients in a way that unleashes these capabilities and resources toward solving problems and changing lives.

Empowerment

Any discussion of strengths-based approaches must also consider empowerment as an instrumental element of the approach. Empowerment, as a term in social work, has evolved over the years. We choose a definition of empowerment that focuses on power; internal, interpersonal, and environmental (Parsons, Gutierrez, & Cox, 1998). According to Parsons, Gutierrez, and Cox (1998),

> In its most positive sense, power is (1) the ability to influence the course of one's life, (2) an expression of self worth, (3) the capacity to work with others to control aspects of public life, and (4) access to the mechanisms of public decision making. When used negatively, though, it can also block opportunities for stigmatized groups, exclude others and their concerns from decision making, and be a way to control others. (p. 8)

Hence, empowerment in practice is a process (Parsons, Gutierrez, and Cox, 1998) firmly grounded in ecological systems and strength-based approaches that focus on gaining power by individuals, families, groups, organizations, or communities. It is based on two related assumptions: (1) all human beings are potentially competent, even in extremely challenging situations, and (2) all human beings are subject to various degrees of powerlessness (Cox & Parsons, 1994, p. 17) and oppression (Freire, 1993). People internalize their sense of powerlessness and oppression in a way that their definition of self in the world is limited, often eliminating any notion that they can act in their own behalf in a positive manner.

An empowerment approach makes practical connections between power and powerlessness. It illuminates how these factors interact to influence clients in their daily life. Empowerment is not achieved through a single intervention, nor is it something that can be "done" to another. Empowerment does not occur through neglect or by simply giving responsibility for life and well-being to the poor or troubled, allowing them to be "free" from government regulation, support, or professional assistance. In other words, empowerment of disenfranchised groups does not occur simply by dismantling systems (such as the welfare system) to allow these groups or individuals to take responsibility for themselves. Hence, empowerment does not preclude helping.

Consistent with our definition, empowerment develops through the approach taken toward helping, not the act of helping itself. Empowerment is a sense of gained or regained power that someone attains in their life that provides the foun-

dation for change in the short term, and stimulates belief in their ability to positive-
ly influence their lives over the long term. Empowerment occurs as a function of
the long-term approach of the practitioner and the professional relationship developed between practitioner and client. One cannot provide an empowering context
through a constant focus on problems, deficits, inadequacies, negative labeling, and
dependency.

The Power of Choice

Choice is an instrumental part of strengths-based and empowerment approaches, by
recognizing that people, because of inherent strengths and capabilities, can make
informed choices about their lives, just like people who are not clients. Practitioners
work toward offering people choices about how they define their lives and problems, the extent to which they want to address their problems, and the means or
mechanisms through which change should occur. Clients become active and instrumental partners in the helping process. They are not passive vessels, waiting for
practitioners to "change them" through some crafty intervention or technique.

We are not talking about the false choices sometimes given to clients by practitioners. For example, clients with substance abuse problems are often told that they
must either abstain or leave treatment. Most practitioners ignore or use as evidence
of denial, client requests to attempt so-called controlled use. If practitioners were
interested in offering true choice, they would work with these clients toward their
controlled-drinking goal in an effort to reduce the potential harm that may result
from their use of substances (Johnson, 2004; van Wormer & Davis, 2003), even if
the practitioner believes that controlled drinking is not possible. Abstinence would
become the goal only when their clients choose to include it as a goal.

Client Engagement as Cultural Competence

Empowerment (choice) occurs through a process of culturally competent client
engagement, created by identifying strengths, generating dialogue targeted at
revealing the extent of people's oppression (Freire, 1993), and respecting their right
to make informed choices in their lives. Accordingly, empowerment is the "trans-
formation from individual and collective powerlessness to personal, political, and
cultural power" (GlenMaye, 1998, p. 29), through a strengths-based relationship
with a professional helper.

Successful application of AMS requires the ability to engage clients in open
and trusting professional relationships. The skills needed to engage clients from different backgrounds and with different personal and cultural histories are what drives
practice; what determines the difference between successful and unsuccessful practice. Advanced client engagement skills allow the practitioner to elicit in-depth,
multi-systemic information in a dialogue between client and practitioner (Johnson,
2004), providing the foundation for strengths-based client empowerment leading to
change.

Earlier, we defined client engagement as a mutual process occurring between clients and practitioners in a professional context, created by practitioners. In other words, creating the professional space and open atmosphere that allows engagement to flourish is the primary responsibility of the practitioner, not the client. Practitioners must have the skills and knowledge to adjust their approach toward specific clients and the client's cultural context and not *vice versa*. Clients do not adjust to us and our beliefs, values, and practices—we adjust to them. When that occurs, the foundation exists for client engagement. By definition, relationships of this nature must be performed in a culturally competent manner. Yet, what does this mean?

Over the last two decades, social work and other helping professions have been concerned with cultural competence in practice (Fong, 2001). Beginning in the late 1970s, the professional literature has been replete with ideas, definitions, and practice models designed to increase cultural awareness and promote culturally appropriate practice methods. Yet, despite the attention given to the issue, there remains confusion about how to define and teach culturally competent practice.

Structural and Historical Systems of Oppression: Who Holds the Power?

Often embedded in laws, policies, and social institutions are oppressive influences such as racism, sexism, homophobia, and classism, to name a few. These structural issues play a significant role in the lives of clients (through maltreatment and discrimination) and in social work practice. How people are treated (or how they internalize historical treatment of self, family, friends, and/or ancestors) shapes how they believe, think, and act in the present. Oppression affects how they perceive that others feel about them, how they view the world and their place in it, and how receptive they are to professional service providers. Therefore, culturally competent practice must consider the impact of structural systems of oppression and injustice on clients, their problems, strengths, and potential for change.

Oppression is a by-product of socially constructed notions of power, privilege, control, and hierarchies of difference. As stated above, it is created and maintained by differences in power. By definition, those who have power can force people to abide by the rules, standards, and actions the powerful deem worthwhile, mandatory, or acceptable. Those who hold power can enforce particular worldviews; deny equal access and opportunity to housing, employment, or health care; define right and wrong, normal and abnormal; and imprison, confine, and/or commit physical, emotional, or mental violence against the powerless (McLaren, 1995; Freire, 1993). Most importantly, power permits the holder to "set the very terms of power" (Appleby, 2001, p. 37). It defines the interaction between the oppressed and the oppressor, and between the social worker and client.

Social institutions and practices are developed and maintained by the dominant culture to meet *its* needs and maintain *its* power. Everything and everybody is judged and classified accordingly. Even when the majority culture develops programs or engages in helping activities, these efforts will not include measures that threaten the dominant group's position at the top of the social hierarchy (Freire, 1993). For example, Kozol (1991) wrote eloquently about how public schools fail by design, while Freire (1993) wrote about how state welfare and private charity provide short-term assistance while ensuring that there are not enough resources to lift people permanently out of poverty.

Oppression is neither an academic nor a theoretical consideration; it is not a faded relic of a bygone era. Racism did not end with the civil rights movement, and sexism was not eradicated by the feminist movement. Understanding how systems of oppression work in people's lives is of paramount importance for every individual and family seeking professional help, including those who belong to the *same* race, gender, and class as the practitioner. No two individuals, regardless of their personal demographics, experience the world in the same way. Often, clients are treated ineffectively by professional helpers who mistakenly believe that people who look or act the same will experience the world in similar ways. These workers base their assumptions about clients on stereotypic descriptions of culture, lifestyle, beliefs, and practices. They take group-level data (i.e., many African American adolescents join gangs because of broken families and poverty) and assume that *all* African American teenagers are gang members from single-parent families. Social work values and ethics demand a higher standard, one that compels us to go beyond stereotypes. Our job is to discover, understand, and utilize personal differences in the assessment and treatment process to benefit clients, not use differences as a way of limiting clients' potential for health and well-being.

We cannot accurately assess or treat people without considering the effects of oppression related to race, ethnicity, culture, sexual preference, gender, or physical/emotional status. We need to understand how oppression influences our clients' beliefs about problems and potential approaches to problem solving, and how it determines what kind of support they can expect to receive if they decide to seek help. For example, despite the widely held belief that chemical dependency is an equal opportunity disease (Gordon, 1993), it is clear that some people are more vulnerable than others. While some of the general themes of chemical dependency may appear universal, each client is unique. That is, an individual's dependency results from personal behavior, culture (including the history of one's culture), past experiences, and family interacting with larger social systems that provide opportunities or impose limits on the individual (Johnson, 2000).

Systems of oppression ensure unequal access to resources for certain individuals, families, and communities. However, while all oppressed people are similar in that they lack the power to define their place in the social hierarchy, oppression based on race, gender, sexual orientation, class, and other social factors is expressed in a variety of ways. Learning about cultural nuances is important in client assessment, treatment planning, and treatment (Lum, 1999). According to Pinderhughes (1989), there is no such thing as culture-free service delivery. Cultural differences between clients and social workers in terms of values, norms, beliefs, attitudes, lifestyles, and life opportunities affect every aspect of practice.

What Is Culture?

Many different concepts of culture are used in social work, sociology, and anthropology. Smelser (1992) considers culture a "system of patterned values, meanings, and beliefs that give cognitive structure to the world, provide a basis for coordinating and controlling human interactions, and constitute a link as the system is transmitted from one generation to another" (p. 11). Geertz (1973) regarded culture as simultaneously a product of and a guide to people searching for organized categories and interpretations that provide a meaningful experiential link to their social life. Building upon these two ideas, in this book we abide by the following definition of culture proposed elsewhere (Johnson, 2000):

> Culture is historical, bound up in traditions and practices passed through generations; memories of events—real or imagined—that define a people and their worldview. (Culture) is viewed as collective subjectivity, or a way of life adopted by a community that ultimately defines their worldview. (p. 121)

Consistent with this definition, the collective subjectivities called culture are pervasive forces in the way people interact, believe, think, feel, and act in their social world. Culture plays a significant role in shaping how people view the world. As a historical force, in part built on ideas, definitions, and events passed through generations, culture also defines people's level of social acceptance by the wider community; shapes how people live, think, and act; and influences how people perceive that others feel about them and how they view the world and their place in it. Thus, it is impossible to understand a client without grasping his or her cultural foundations.

Cultural Competence

As stated earlier, over the years many different ideas and definitions of what constitutes culturally competent practice have developed, as indicated by the growth of the professional literature since the late 1970s. To date, focus has primarily been placed in two areas: (1) the need for practitioners to be aware or their own cultural beliefs, ideas, and identities leading to cultural sensitivity, and (2) learning factual and descriptive information about various ethnic and racial groups based mostly on group-level survey data and analyses. Fong (2001) suggests that culture is often considered "tangential" to individual functioning and not central to the client's functioning (p. 5).

To address this issue, Fong (2001) builds on Lum's (1999) culturally competent practice model that focuses on four areas: (1) cultural awareness, (2) knowledge acquisition, (3) skill development, and (4) inductive learning. Besides inductive learning, Lum's model places focuses mainly on practitioners in perpetual self-awareness, gaining knowledge about cultures, and skill building. While these are important ideas for cultural competence, Fong (2001) calls for a shift in thinking and practice, "to provide a culturally competent service focused solely on the client rather than the social worker and what he or she brings to the awareness of ethnicity" (p. 5). Fong (2001) suggests an "extension" (p. 6) of Lum's model by turning the focus of each of the four elements away from the practitioner toward the client. For example, cultural awareness changes from a practitioner focus to "the social worker's understanding and the identification of the critical cultural values important to the client system and to themselves" (p. 6). This change allows Fong (2001) to remain consistent with the stated definition of culturally competent practice, insisting that practitioners

> . . . operating from an empowerment, strengths, and ecological framework, provide services, conduct assessments, and implement interventions that are reflective of the clients' cultural values and norms, congruent with their natural help-seeking behaviors, and inclusive of existing indigenous solutions. (p. 1)

While we agree with the idea that "to be culturally competent is to know the cultural values of the client-system and to use them in planning and implementing services" (Fong, 2001, p. 6), we want to make this shift the main point of a culturally competent model of client engagement. That is, beyond what should or must occur, we believe that professional education and training must focus on the skills of culturally competent client engagement that are necessary to make this happen; a model that places individual client cultural information at the center of practice. We agree with Fong (2001) that having culturally sensitive or culturally aware practitioners is not nearly enough. Practitioner self-awareness and knowledge of different cultures does not constitute cultural competence. We strive to find a method for reaching this worthy goal.

The central issue revolves around practitioners participating in inductive learning and the skills of grounded theory. In other words, regardless of practitioner beliefs, awarenesses, or sensitivities, their job is to learn about and understand their client's world, and "ground" their theory of practice in the cultural context of their client. They develop a unique theory of human behavior in a multi-systemic context for every client. Culturally competent client engagement does not happen by assessing the extent to which client lives "fit" within existing theory and knowledge about reality, most of which is middle-class and Eurocentric at its core. Cultural competence (Johnson, 2004)

> . . . *begins* with learning about different cultures, races, personal circumstances, and structural mechanisms of oppression. It *occurs* when practitioners master the interpersonal skills needed to move beyond general descriptions of a specific culture or race to learn specific individual, family, group, or community interpretations of culture, ethnicity, and race. The culturally competent practitioner knows that within each culture are individually interpreted and practiced thoughts, beliefs, and behaviors that may or may not be consistent with group-level information. That is, there is tremendous diversity within groups, as well as between them. Individuals are unique unto themselves, not simply interchangeable members of a specific culture, ethnicity, or race who natu-

rally abide by the group-level norms often taught in graduate and undergraduate courses on human diversity. (p. 105)

Culturally competent client engagement revolves around the practitioner's ability to create a relationship, through the professional use of self, based in true dialogue (Freire, 1993; Johnson, 2004). We define dialogue as "a joint endeavor, developed between people (in this case, practitioner and client) that move clients from their current state of hopelessness to a more hopeful, motivated position in their world" (Johnson, 2004, p. 97). Elsewhere (Johnson, 2004), we detailed a model of culturally competent engagement based on Freire's (1993) definitions of oppression, communication, dialogue, practitioner self-work, and the ability to exhibit worldview respect, hope, humility, trust, and empathy.

To investigate culture in a competent manner is to take a comprehensive look into people's worldviews—to discover what they believe about the world and their place in it. It goes beyond race and ethnicity (although these are important issues) into how culture determines thoughts, feelings, and behaviors in daily life. This includes what culture says about people's problems; culturally appropriate strengths and resources; the impact of gender on these issues; and what it means to seek professional help (Leigh, 1998).

The larger questions to be answered are how clients uniquely and individually interpret their culture; how their beliefs, attitudes, and behaviors are shaped by that interpretation, and how these cultural beliefs and practices affect daily life and determine lifestyle in the context of the larger community. Additionally, based on their cultural membership, beliefs, and practices, practitioners need to discover the potential and real barriers faced by clients in the world. Many clients, because they are part of non-majority cultures face issues generated by social systems of oppression such as racism, sexism, homophobia, and ethnocentrism that expose them to limitations and barriers that others do not face.

What is the value of culturally competent client engagement? Helping clients discuss their attitudes, beliefs, and behaviors in the context of their culture—including their religious or spiritual belief systems—offers valuable information about their worldview, sense of social and spiritual connection, and/or practical involvement in their social world. Moreover, establishing connections between their unique interpretation of their culture and their daily life provides vital clues about people's belief systems, attitudes, expectations (social construction of reality), and explanation of behaviors that cannot be understood outside the context of their socially constructed interpretation of culture.

A Cautionary Note

It is easy to remember to ask about culture when clients are obviously different (i.e., different races, countries of origin, etc.). However, many practitioners forgo cultural investigation with clients they consider to have the same cultural background as the practitioner. For example, the search for differences between European

Americans with Christian beliefs—if the social worker shares these characteristics—gets lost in mutual assumptions, based on the misguided belief that there are no important differences between them. The same is often true when clients and practitioners come from the same racial, cultural, or lifestyle backgrounds (i.e., African American practitioner and client, gay practitioner and gay client, etc.). Culturally competent practice means that practitioners are always interested in people's individual interpretation of their culture and their subjective definitions of reality, whether potential differences are readily apparent or not. Practitioners must be diligent to explore culture with clients who appear to be from the same background as the practitioner, just as they would with people who are obviously from different cultural, racial, ethnic, or religious backgrounds.

Multiple Theories & Methods

No single theory, model, or method is best suited to meet the needs of all clients (Miley, O'Melia, & DuBois, 2004). Consistent with this statement, one of the hallmarks of AMS is the expectation that practitioners must determine which theory, model, or method will best suit a particular client. Choosing from a range of approaches and interventions, AMS practitioners develop the skills and abilities to: (1) determine, based on the client's life, history, culture, and style, which treatment approach (theory and/or method) would best suit their needs and achieve the desired outcome, (2) determine which modality or modalities (individual, family, group treatment, etc.) will best meet the need of their clients, and (3) conduct treatment according to their informed clinical decisions.

Over the last 20 years or so, graduate social work education has trended toward practice specialization through concentration-based curricula. Many graduate schools of social work build on the generalist foundation by insisting that students focus on learning specific practice models or theories (disease, cognitive-behavioral, psychoanalysis, etc.) and/or specific practice methods (individual, family, group, etc.), often at the exclusion of other methods or models. For example, students often enter the field intent on doing therapy with individuals, say, from a cognitive-behavioral approach only.

This trend encourages practitioners to believe that one approach or theory best represents the "Truth." Truth, in this sense, is the belief that one theory or approach works best for most people, most of the time. It helps create a practice scenario that leads practitioners to use their chosen approach with every client they treat. Therefore, practice becomes a process of the practitioner forcing clients to adjust to the practitioner's beliefs and expectations about the nature of problems, the course of treatment, and definition of positive versus negative outcomes. From this perspective, what is best for clients is determined by what the practitioner believes is best, not what clients believe is in their best interest.

Some practitioners take their belief in the Truth of a particular theory or method to extremes. They believe that one model or theory works best for all people, all the time. We found this to be common in the family therapy field, whereby some true believers insist that everyone needs family therapy—so that is all they offer. What's worse is that many of these same practitioners know and use only one particular family therapy theory and model. The "true believer" approach can cause problems, especially for clients. For example, when clients do not respond to treatment, instead of looking to other approaches, true believers simply prescribe more of the method that did not work in the first place. If a more intensive application of the method does not work, then the client's "lack of readiness" for treatment, resistance, or denial becomes the culprit. These practitioners usually give little thought to their practice approach or personal style and its impact on client "readiness" for treatment. They fail to examine the role their personal style, beliefs, attitudes, and practices have in creating the context that led to clients not succeeding in treatment.

Each practice theory and model has a relatively unique way of defining client problems, practitioner method and approach, interventions, and what constitutes successful outcome. For practitioners to believe that one theory or model is true, even if only for most people, they must believe in the universality of problems, methods and approaches, interventions, and successful outcome criteria. This contradicts the definition of theory. While being far from a concrete representation of the truth, a theory is a set of myths, expectations, guesses, and conjectures about what might be true (Best & Kellner, 1991). A theory is hypothetical; a set of ideas and explanations that need proving. No single theory can explain everything. According to Popper (1994), a theory ". . . always remains guesswork, and there is no theory that is not beset with problems" (p. 157). As such, treatment specialization can—although not always—encourage people to believe they have found the Truth where little truth exists.

Practitioners using an AMS perspective come to believe that some element of every established practice model, method, or theory may be helpful. Accordingly, every model, method, or theory can be adapted and used in a multi-systemic practice framework. As an AMS practitioner, one neither accepts any single model fully, nor disregards a model entirely if there is potential for helping a client succeed in a way that is compatible with professional social work values and ethics. These practitioners hone their critical thinking skills (Gambrill, 1997, 1990) and apply them in practice, particularly as it pertains to treatment theories, models, and methods. In the context of evidence-based practice (Cournoyer, 2004; Gibbs, 2003), sharpened critical thinking skills allow practitioners to closely read and evaluate practice theories, research, or case reports to recognize the strengths, weakness, and contradictions in theories, models, and/or policy related to social work practice.

Informed Eclecticism

The goal of AMS is for practitioners to develop an approach we call *informed eclecticism.* Informed eclecticism allows the use of multiple methods, interventions, and approaches in the context of practice that: (1) is held together by a perspective or approach that provides consistency, that makes practice choices in a way that makes sense in a particular client's life; and (2) is based, whenever possible, on the latest evidence about its efficacy with particular problems and particular clients. While it is often best to rely on empirical evidence, this data is in its infancy. AMS does not preclude the use of informed practice wisdom and personal creativity in developing intervention plans and approaches. It is up to practitioners to ensure that any treatment based in practice wisdom or that is creatively generated be discussed with colleagues, supervisors, or consultants to ensure theoretical consistency and that it fits within the code of professional ethics.

Informed eclecticism is different from the routine definition of eclecticism—the use of whatever theory, model, or method works best for their clients. While this is the goal of AMS practice specifically and social work practice in general (Timberlake, Farber, & Sabatino, 2004), it is an elusive goal indeed. Informed eclecticism often gets lost in a practitioner's quest to find something that "works." According to Gambrill (1997), eclecticism is "the view that we should adopt whatever theories or methodologies is useful in inquiry, no matter what their source and without worry about their consistency" (p. 93). The most important word in Gambrill's statement is "consistency." While there are practitioners who have managed to develop a consistent, organized, and holistic version of informed eclecticism, this is not the norm.

Too often, uninformed eclecticism resembles the following. A practitioner specializes by modality (individual therapy) and uses a variety of modality-specific ideas and practices in his work with clients; changing ideas and tactics when the approach he normally uses does not "work." This often leaves the practitioner searching (mostly in vain) for the magic intervention—what "works." Moreover, while uninformed eclectic practitioners use interventions from various "schools," they remain primarily wedded to one modality. Hence, they end up confusing themselves and their clients as they search for the "right" approach, rarely looking beyond their chosen modality, and therefore, never actually looking outside of their self-imposed, theoretical cage.

For example, an uninformed eclectic practitioner specializing in individual therapy may try a cognitive approach, a client-centered approach, a Freudian approach, or a behavioral approach. A family therapy specialist may use a structural, strategic, or solution-focused approach. However, in the end, little changes. These practitioners still believe that their clients need individual or family treatment. They rarely consider potentially useful ideas and tactics taken from different modalities that could be used instead of, or in combination with, an individual or family approach, mostly because they base treatment decisions on their chosen modality.

While informed eclecticism is the goal, most find it difficult to find consistency when trying to work from a variety of models at the same time. The informed eclectic practitioners, through experience and empirical evidence, have a unifying approach that serves as the basis for using different models or methods. What is important, according to clinical outcome research, is the consistency of approach in helping facilitate successful client outcome (Gaston, 1990; Miller & Rollnick, 2002; Harper & Lantz, 1996). Trying to be eclectic makes consistency (and treatment success), quite difficult. What uninformed eclecticism lacks is the framework needed to gain a holistic and comprehensive understanding of the client in the context of his or her life, history, and multiple environments that leads naturally to culturally consistent treatment and intervention decisions. AMS, as it is described here, provides such a framework. It is holistic, integrative, ecological, and based in the latest empirical evidence. It is an inclusive framework that bases treatment decisions on a multi- systemic assessment of specific client history and culture. It is designed, whenever possible, to capitalize on client strengths, be consistent with culturally specific help-seeking behavior, and utilize existing or formulated community-based and/or natural support systems in the client's environment.

Defining Multi-Systemic Client Information

In this section we specifically discuss the different dimensions that comprise AMS practice. This is a general look at what constitutes multi-systemic client life information. There are six levels of information that, when integrated into a life history of clients, demonstrates how multiple theories, models, and approaches can be applied to better understand, assess, and treat clients or client-systems. Generally, the six dimensions (biological, psychological, family, religious/spiritual/existential, social/environmental, and macro) encompass range of information needed to complete a comprehensive, multi-systemic assessment, treatment, and intervention plan with client-systems of all sizes and configurations.

1. Biological Dimension

AMS practitioners need to understand what some have called the "mind-body connection," or the links between social/emotional, behavioral, and potential biological or genetic issues that may be, at least in part, driving the problems presented by clients in practice. As scientific evidence mounts regarding the biological and genetic sources of personal troubles (i.e., some mental illness, etc.), it grows imperative for well-trained AMS practitioners to apply this knowledge in everyday work with clients (Ginsberg, Nackerud, & Larrison, 2004). The responsibility for understanding biology and physical health goes well beyond those working in direct health care practice settings (i.e., hospital, HIV, or hospice practice settings). Issues pertaining to physical health confront practitioners in all practice settings.

For example, practitioners working in mental health settings are confronted daily with issues pertaining to human biology; the sources and determinants of mental illness, differential uses of psychotropic medication, and often, the role played in client behavior by proper nutrition, appropriate health care, and even physical rest. In foster care and/or family preservation, practitioners also confront the effects of parental abuses (i.e., fetal alcohol syndrome [FAS]), medication management, and child/adolescent physical and biological development issues.

Beyond learning about the potential biological or physical determinants of various client troubles, having a keen understanding of the potential physical and health risks associated with various behaviors and/or lifestyles places practitioners in the position of intervening to save lives. For example, practitioners working with substance abusing or chemically dependent clients must understand drug pharmacology—especially drug-mixing—to predict potentially life-threatening physical withdrawal effects and/or to prevent intentional or unintentional harm caused by drug overdose (Johnson, 2004).

AMS requires that practitioners keep current with the latest information about human biology, development, genetics, and potential associated health risks facing clients and client-systems in practice. With that knowledge, practitioners can include this information during client assessment, treatment planning, and intervention strategies. It also requires practitioners to know the limits of professional responsibility. That is, social workers are not physicians and should never offer medical advice or guidance that is not supported by properly trained physicians. Therefore, AMS practitioners utilize the appropriate medical professionals as part of assessment, planning, and intervention processes with all clients.

2. Psychological/Emotional Dimension

AMS practitioners need a working knowledge of the ways that psychological and emotional functioning are intertwined with clients' problems and strengths, how issues from this dimension contribute to the way their client or client-system interacts with self and others in their environment, and how their environments influence their psychological and emotional functioning. There are several important skill sets that practitioners must develop to consider issues in this dimension. First, being able to recognize potential problems through a mental screening examination is a skill necessary to all practitioners. Also, having a keen understanding of the *Diagnostic and Statistical Manual of Mental Disorders* (DSM) (American Psychological Association, 2000), including the multi-axial diagnostic process, and recognition of the limits of this tool in the overall multi-systemic assessment process is instrumental. Especially critical is the ability to recognize co-occurring disorders (Johnson, 2004). It is also valuable to learn the Person-in-Environment (PIE) assessment system (Karls & Wandrei, 1994a, 1994b), a diagnostic model developed specifically for social workers to incorporate environmental influences.

In addition to understanding how psychology and emotion affects client mood and behavior, AMS practitioners also know how to employ different theories and models used for treating psychological and emotional functioning problems in the context of a client's multi-systemic assessment and treatment plan. This includes methods of treating individuals, families, and groups. Depending on the client's multi-systemic assessment, each of these modalities or some combination of modalities is appropriate for people with problems in this dimension.

3. Family Dimension

The family is the primary source of socialization, modeling, and nurturing of children. Hence, the family system has a significant impact on people's behavior, and people's behavior has significant impact on the health and well-being of their family system (Johnson, 2004). By integrating a family systems perspective into AMS, practitioners will often be able to make sense of behavior attitudes, beliefs, and values that would otherwise be difficult to understand or explain.

For our purposes, a family is defined as a group of people—regardless of their actual blood or legal relationship—whom clients consider to be members of their family (Johnson, 2004). This definition is designed to privilege clients' perceptions and subjective construction of reality and avoid disagreements over who is or is not in someone's family. So, if a client refers to a neighbor as "Uncle Joe," then that perception represents their reality. What good would it do to argue otherwise? Just as in client engagement discussed earlier, AMS practitioners seek to understand and embrace their client's unique definition of family, rather than imposing a rigid standard that may not fit their perceived reality. This is especially important when dealing with gay and lesbian clients. The law may not recognize gay or lesbian marriage, but AMS practitioners must, if that is the nature of the client's relationship and consistent with their belief system.

It is important to have a working knowledge of different theories and approaches to assessing and treating families and couples, as well as the ability to construct three-generation genograms to help conceptualize family systems and characterize the relationships that exist within the family system and between the family and its environment. Family treatment requires unique skills, specialized post-graduate training, and regular supervision before a practitioner can master the methods and call herself a "family therapist." However, the journey toward mastery is well worth it. Family treatment can be among the most effective and meaningful treatment modalities, often used in conjunction with other modalities (individual and/or group treatment), or as the primary treatment method.

4. Religious/Spiritual/Existential Dimension

Practitioners, students, and social work educators are often wary of exploring issues related to religion and spirituality in practice or the classroom. While there are exceptions, this important dimension often goes unexamined. Exploring people's religious beliefs and/or the tenets of their faith, even if they do not appear to have faith of spiritual beliefs, as they pertain to people's subjective definition of self in relation to the world is an important part of AMS practice.

How clients view themselves in relation to others and their world provides an interesting window into the inner workings of their individual interpretation of culture. The extent that clients have internalized messages (positive, negative, and/or neutral) about their behavior from their faith community or personal spiritual belief systems can lead to an understanding of why people approach their lives and others in the ways they do. Moreover, much can be learned, based on these beliefs, about people's belief in the potential for change, how change occurs, and whom is best suited to help in that change process (if anyone at all), especially as it relates to the many moral and religious messages conveyed about people with problems.

Examination of this dimension goes beyond discovering which church or synagogue clients attend. It is designed to learn how and by what means clients define themselves and their lives in their worlds. What tenets they use to justify their lives, and how these tenets either support their current lives or can be used to help lead them toward change. There is much to be learned about client culture, how people interpret their culture in daily life, and how they view their life in their personal context from an examination of their religious or spiritual beliefs.

Moreover, religious and spiritual belief systems can also be a source of strength and support when considered in treatment plans. For example, while many clients may benefit from attendance at a community support group (i.e., Alcoholics Anonymous, Overeaters Anonymous, etc.) or professional treatment, some will benefit even more from participation in groups and events through local houses of worship. In our experience, many clients unable to succeed in professional treatment or support groups found success through a connection or reconnection with organizations that share their faith, whatever that faith may be.

5. Social/Environmental Dimension

Beyond the individual and family, AMS practitioners look to the client's community, including the physical environment, for important clues to help with engagement, assessment, and intervention planning. People live in communities comprised of three different types: (1) location (neighborhoods, cities, and rural or urban villages), (2) identification (religion, culture, race, etc.), and (3) affiliation (group memberships, subcultures, professional, political/ideological groups, etc.). There are five subdimensions that comprise the social/environmental dimension and incorporate the three types of communities listed above (Johnson, 2004):

1. Local community.   This includes learning about physical environment, living conditions, a person's fit within her community, neighborhoods, where and how people live on a daily basis, and how they believe they are treated and/or accepted by community members and the community's power structure (i.e., the police, etc.).

2. Cultural context.   This includes learning about clients' larger culture, their individual interpretation of culture, and how it drives or influences their daily life. Also included here is an exploration of histories of oppression and discrimination (individual, family, and community) and a client's subcultural group membership (i.e., drug culture, gang culture, etc.).

3. Social class.   Often overlooked by practitioners, "information about people's social class is directly related to information about their families, the goodness-of-fit between the person and environment, and the strengths, resources, and/or barriers in their communities" (Johnson, 2004, p. 226). Some believe that no other demographic factor explains so extensively the differences between people and/or groups (Lipsitz, 1997; Davis & Proctor, 1989). Social class represents a combination of income, education, occupation, prestige, and community. It encompasses how these factors affect people's relative wealth and access to power and opportunity (Johnson, 2004).

4. Social/relational.   Human beings are social creatures who define themselves in relation to others (Johnson, 2004). Therefore, it is necessary to know something about people's ability to relate to others in their social environment. This investigation includes loved ones, friends, peers, supervisors, teachers, and others that they relate to in their daily life.

5. Legal history and involvement.   Obviously, this subdimension includes information about involvement with the legal system, by the client, family members, and friends and peers. More than recording a simple demographic history, seek to discover their feelings, attitudes, and beliefs about themselves, their place in the world, and how their brushes with the law fit into or influence their worldview.

6. Community resources.   Investigate the nature and availability of organizational support, including the role of social service organizations, politics, and your presence as a social worker in a client's life. For example, can clients find a program to serve their needs, or what does seeing a social worker mean within their community or culture? What are the conditions of the schools and the influence of churches, neighborhood associations, and block clubs? More importantly, what is the prevailing culture of the local environment? Are neighbors supportive or afraid of each other, and can a client expect to reside in the present situation and receive the support needed to change?

Be sure to include the professional helping system in this subdimension. Practitioners, their agencies, and the policies that assist or impede the professional helping process join with client-systems as part of the overall system in treatment. In other words, we must consider ourselves as part of the system—we do not stand outside in objective observation. This includes practitioner qualities and styles, agency policies, broader policies related to specific populations, and reimbursement policies, including managed care. All of these factors routinely influence the extent to which clients receive help, how clients are perceived in the helping system and, in the case of reimbursement policies, the method of treatment clients are eligible to receive regardless of how their multi-systemic assessment turns out.

Familiarity with various theories and models of community provide the keys to understanding the role of the social, physical, political, and economic environment in an individual's life. Community models look at the broader environment and its impact on people. Clients or client-systems with issues located in this dimension often respond well to group and family treatment methods. Occasionally, practitioners will be required to intervene at the local neighborhood or community level through organizing efforts and/or personal or political advocacy. For example:

> I (Johnson) was treating a client in individual and occasional family treatment when it was discovered that the daughter had been molested by a neighbor. The parents had not reported the molestation. I soon learned that this neighbor was rumored to have molested several young girls in the neighborhood and that nobody was willing to report the molestations. I urged my client to organize a neighborhood meeting of all involved parents at her home. I served as the group facilitator for an intense meeting

that ultimately built the community support needed to involve law enforcement. Within days, all of the parents in this group met with law enforcement. The perpetrator was arrested, convicted, and sentenced to life imprisonment.

6. Macro Dimension

AMS practitioners do not stop looking for relevant client information at the local level. They also look for clues in the way that macro issues influence clients, their problems, and potential for change. Knowledge of various laws (local, state, and national) are critical, as well as an understanding of how various social policies are interpreted and enforced in a particular client's life. For example, AMS requires an understanding of how child welfare policies affect the life of a chemically dependent mother, how healthcare policy affects a family's decisions about seeking medical treatment for their children, or how local standards of hygiene or cleanliness affect a family's status and acceptance in their community.

Issues to consider at this level also include public sentiment, stereotypes, and mechanisms of oppression that play a significant role in the lives of people who are not Caucasian, male, middle-class (or more affluent) citizens. Racism, classism, homophobia, and sexism, to name a few, are real threats to people who are attempting to live a "normal" life. An AMS practitioner must understand this reality and learn from clients what their individual perceptions are of these mechanisms and how they affect their problems and potential for change. The macro dimension involves issues such as housing, employment, and public support, along with the dynamics of the criminal justice system. For example, if clients have been arrested for domestic violence, what is the chance they will get fair and just legal representation? If they have been convicted and served jail or prison sentences, what are the chances they will have a reasonable chance of finding sufficient employment upon release?

These issues can be addressed in individual, family, or group treatments. Often, group treatment is an effective way to address issues clients struggle with at the macro level. Group treatment provides clients a way to address these issues in the context of mutual social support and a sense of belonging, helping them realize that they are not alone in their struggles (Yalom, 1995). AMS practitioners also recognize the need for political advocacy and community organizing methods for clients who present with consistent struggles with issues at the macro level.

Summary

The hallmark of AMS is its reliance on and integration of multi-systemic client information into one comprehensive assessment, treatment, and intervention plan. It incorporates knowledge, skills, and values from multiple sources, and relies on various sources of knowledge to paint a holistic picture of people's lives, struggles, strengths and resources, and potentials for change. Practitioners need a current working knowledge of human behavior, social systems theories, the latest social research and practice evaluation results, the impact of public laws and policies, as well as the skills and abilities to plan and implement treatment approaches as needed, in a manner consistent with our definition of informed eclecticism.

Many students new to AMS start out confused because the requirements seem so diverse and complicated. However, as you will see in the case presentations to follow, an organized and efficient practitioner who has learned to think and act multi-systemically can gather large amounts of critically important information about a client in a relatively short period. For this to happen, you must have a deep understanding of various theories, models, and practice approaches that address the various systemic levels considered and be willing to accept that no single model is completely right or wrong. It is always easier to latch on to one model and "go with it." However, the goal of practice is not to be correct or to promote your own ease and comfort, but to develop an assessment and treatment plan that is right for each client, whether or not you would ever use it in your own life. Social work practice is not about the social worker, but the client. It is important never to lose sight of this fact.

Bibliography

American Psychiatric Association (2000). *Diagnostic and statistical manual of mental disorders* (4th ed., TR). Washington, DC: Author.

Appleby, G. A. (2001). Dynamics of oppression and discrimination. In G. A. Appleby, E. Colon, & J. Hamilton (eds.), *Diversity, oppression, and social functioning: Person-in-environment assessment and intervention.* Boston: Allyn and Bacon.

Best, S., & Kellner, D. (1991). *Postmodern theory: Critical interrogations.* New York: Guilford Press.

Cournoyer, B. R. (2004). *The evidence-based social work skills book.* Boston: Allyn and Bacon.

Cox, E. O., & Parsons, R. J. (1994). *Empowerment-oriented social work practice with the elderly.* Pacific Grove, CA: Brooks/Cole.

Davis, L. E., & Proctor, E. K. (1989). *Race, gender, and class: Guidelines for practice with individuals, families, and groups.* Englewood Cliffs, NJ: Prentice-Hall.

Derezotes, D. S. (2000). *Advanced generalist social work practice.* Thousand Oaks, CA: Sage.

Fong, R. (2001). Culturally competent social work practice: Past and present. In R. Fong & S. Furuto (eds.), *Culturally competent practice: Skills, interventions, and evaluations.* Boston: Allyn and Bacon.

Freire, P. (1993). *Pedagogy of the oppressed.* New York: Continuum.

Gambrill, E. (1997). *Social work practice: A critical thinker's guide.* New York: Oxford University Press.

Gambrill, E. (1990). *Critical thinking in clinical practice.* San Francisco: Jossey-Bass.

Gaston, L. (1990). The concept of the alliance and its role in psychotherapy: Theoretical and empirical considerations. *Psychotherapy, 27,* 143–153.

Geertz, C. (1973). *The interpretation of cultures.* New York: Basic Books.

Germain, C. B., & Gitterman, A. (1996). *The life model of social work practice* (2nd ed.). New York: Columbia University Press.

Germain, C. B., & Gitterman, A. (1980). *The ecological model of social work practice.* New York: Columbia University Press.

Gibbs, L. E. (2003). *Evidence-based practice for the helping professions: A practical guide with integrated multimedia*. Pacific Grove, CA: Brooks/Cole.

Ginsberg, L., Nackerud, L., & Larrison, C. R. (2004). *Human biology for social workers: Development, ecology, genetics, and health*. Boston: Allyn and Bacon.

GlenMaye, L. (1998). Empowerment of women. In L. M. Gutierrez, R. J. Parsons, & E. O. Cox (eds.), *Empowerment in social work practice: A sourcebook*. Pacific Grove, CA: Brooks/Cole.

Gordon, J. U. (1993). A culturally specific approach to ethnic minority young adults. In E. M. Freeman (ed.), *Substance abuse treatment: A family systems perspective*. Newbury Park, CA: Sage.

Greif, G. L. (1986). The ecosystems perspective "meets the press." *Social Work, 31,* 225–226.

Harper, K. V., & Lantz, J. (1996). *Cross-cultural practice: Social work practice with diverse populations*. Chicago: Lyceum Books.

Johnson, J. L. (2004). *Fundamentals of substance abuse practice*. Pacific Grove, CA: Brooks/Cole.

Johnson, J. L. (2000). *Crossing borders—Confronting history: Intercultural adjustment in a post-Cold War world*. Lanham, MD: University Press of America.

Karls, J., & Wandrei, K. (1994a). *Person-in-environment system: The PIE classification system for functioning problems*. Washington, DC: NASW.

Karls, J., & Wandrei, K. (1994b). *PIE manual: Person-in-environment system: The PIE classification system for social functioning*. Washington, DC: NASW.

Kozol, J. (1991). *Savage inequalities: Children in America's schools*. New York: Crown Publishers.

Leigh, J. W. (1998). *Communicating for cultural competence*. Boston: Allyn & Bacon.

Lipsitz, G. (1997). Class and class consciousness: Teaching about social class in public universities. In A. Kumar (ed.), *Class issues*. New York: New York University Press.

Longres, J. F. (2000). *Human behavior in the social environment* (3rd ed.). Itasca, IL: F. E. Peacock.

Lum, D. (1999). *Culturally competent practice*. Pacific Grove, CA: Brooks/Cole.

McLaren, P. (1995). *Critical pedagogy and predatory culture: Oppositional politics in a postmodern era*. London: Routledge.

Miley, K. K., O'Melia, M., & DuBois, B. (2004). *Generalist social work practice: An empowerment approach*. Boston: Allyn and Bacon.

Miller, W. R., & Rollnick, S. (2002). *Motivational interviewing: Preparing people to change addictive behavior* (2nd ed.). New York: Guilford Press.

Mills, C. W. (1959). *The sociological imagination*. New York: Oxford University Press.

Parsons, R. J., Gutierrez, L. M., & Cox, E. O. (1998). A model for empowerment practice. In L. M. Gutierrez, R. J. Parsons, & E. O. Cox (eds.), *Empowerment in social work practice: A sourcebook*. Pacific Grove, CA: Brooks/Cole.

Pinderhughes, E. (1989). *Understanding race, ethnicity, and power*. New York: Free Press.

Popper, K. R. (1994). *The myth of the framework: In defense of science and rationality*. Edited by M. A. Notturno. New York: Routledge.

Saleebey, D. (2002). *The strengths perspective in social work practice* (3rd ed.). Boston: Allyn and Bacon.

Smelser, N. J. (1992). Culture: Coherent or incoherent. In R. Munch & N. J. Smelser (eds.), *Theory of culture*. Berkeley, CA: University of California Press.

Timberlake, E. M., Farber, M. Z., & Sabatino, C. A. (2002). *The general method of social work practice: McMahon's generalist perspective* (4th ed.). Boston: Allyn and Bacon.

van Wormer, K., & Davis, D. R. (2003). *Addiction treatment: A strengths perspective*. Pacific Grove, CA: Brooks/Cole.

Yalom, I. (1995). *The theory and practice of group psychotherapy* (4th ed.). New York: Basic Books.

2

Bob and Phil

Joan M. Borst

I first met Bob in the local HIV/AIDS clinic moments after he discovered that his partner, Phil, was in late stage HIV. It was clear that Phil was not going to live, and Bob was in significant crisis. This case began during the time when the so-called AIDS cocktail drugs were unavailable, making an HIV and AIDS diagnosis a certain and relatively quick death sentence. As you will read, I spent many years on the frontlines, dealing with this dreadful disease and the devastating consequences it had on those with the disease, along with their family, friends, and loved ones. The following case examines HIV/AIDS and its devastating affect on people and communities.

Bob and Phil: Client Presentation

Bob was a 32-year-old, attractive, and sharply dressed gay white male. He grew up in a lower-middle class family with his mother, father, and three siblings—one older brother and two younger sisters. About ten years earlier, Bob and Phil met and fell in love. Soon after, they began living together as a couple. This caused a significant rift between both partners and their families. However, they were young, happy, financially well-off, and in love. The future was indeed bright and full of promise and hope despite the problems with their families and others who thought they were "sinners" because they were gay.

Bob and Phil enjoyed a comfortable lifestyle. Both men had good jobs and good incomes. Phil was a high school teacher for 20 years and Bob worked in management for a local manufacturing company. Despite their time together and the quality of life, as many couples do, Bob and Phil had broken up twice during their 10-year relationship. When they broke up, Bob routinely moved out of the house. The first break-up lasted approximately one month and the second, two weeks. Even when they were apart, Bob always knew that they would eventually get back together, which they did each time. Because of his certainty about their relationship, Bob never dated outside the relationship. He was sure that Phil had maintained the same level of commitment. They had recently moved to the local area after his company transferred Bob.

Bob was a highly successful manager in a local manufacturing business. He worked for this company for 12 years, steadily moving through the managerial ranks. His peers and upper management respected Bob's work ethic and performance. He routinely worked 60 hours per week, supervising four employees, directing multi-level sales campaigns, and managing a $500,000 budget. He was a highly respected asset for his company.

I first met Bob at a local HIV clinic. I became his primary counselor on the day that Bob called "the worst day of my life." Working in this field, I was used to meeting people under such dreadful circumstances. While Bob's case was unique in that Bob and Phil were unique individuals, I had seen the heartbreak and betrayal many times in the past. In that sense, their case was all too common in this field of practice.

Questions

Before reading further, assume that you are the social worker responsible for engaging Bob for services at the local HIV/AIDS clinic. HIV/AIDS is a pervasive problem that brings with it a constellation of issues and problems unique to this population. Before working with Bob, you must know the current literature on HIV/AIDS and treating people associated with this disease.

1. Examine the professional literature regarding HIV/AIDS. What does the literature state about the various issues and problems brought on by this disease? Since you are working in an HIV/AIDS clinic, describe the medical and healthcare issues involved with clients associated with HIV/AIDS.

2. If this were your case, what strategies would you use to engage Bob at the clinic? What does the practice literature say about engaging and working with people in Bob's difficult position, having a life partner diagnosed with AIDS?

HIV/AIDS

In one way or another, the Human Immunodeficiency Virus (HIV) affects nearly everyone. If you do not have HIV, perhaps you know someone with HIV. If you do not know someone with HIV, you probably know someone who does. HIV is no longer a disease that affects "those" people. HIV-positive people live and work in every community and at every level and strata of American life. It is present in every state and most countries. Therefore, social workers must prepare to work with people affected and infected with HIV. Moreover, since HIV leads to AIDS, our profession needs to be among the leaders in helping people who are infected with the disease at all stages of the illness and those people close to the person with the disease.

In the field of HIV/AIDS practice, social workers help clients learn to cope with the diagnosis of this chronic illness and link them with needed support and medical services in their community. As a pervasive and chronic illness, HIV challenges patients and loved ones at every level imaginable: spiritually, physically, emotionally, and financially. While there are now medications available to extend the life of HIV-positive people, it remains a chronic and ultimately fatal disease. Hence, people living with HIV face many challenges in the short- and long-term.

As in any medical setting, social workers must learn about the disease if they hope to help people through their crisis and longer-term struggles. While clients will always know more about their experiences (not the disease necessarily) than practitioners will, we must know the "basics" about the disease. Practitioners cannot expect clients to teach them about HIV. What clients need is to be a client, express their feelings, and learn to cope with this life-changing issue. We have the responsibility to learn all we can about HIV and its many unique emotional, physical, spiritual, and social consequences (Holt, Houg, & Romano, 1999).

The Disease

HIV is a human virus that first appeared in the United States in the early 1980s (Averitt, 2000). HIV/AIDS was particularly frightening because people were dying from a disease that few knew anything about. It took time for scientists to learn what caused the disease, how the infection spread, and how to help people remain safe from infection. Much of society found relief through the belief that HIV and AIDS only affected gay men. This wrongheaded assumption, based mainly in bias, fear, and hatred of gay men, stalled the important local and national efforts required to understand HIV/AIDS and prevent its spread. It also stalled the political will by the U.S. Government to make HIV/AIDS research and treatment a priority.

Not until heterosexuals and famous people (i.e., Rock Hudson) began turning up with HIV, did efforts to understand and prevent the disease begin on a widespread basis. Beginning with the efforts of U.S. Surgeon General Dr. C. Everett Koops in the 1980s, scientists and the public soon learned that HIV/AIDS was far more than a gay disease. By the late 1980s, most people knew that HIV was spread by blood to blood contact through blood transfusions, breast milk, and sexual contact involving the exchange of bodily fluids. HIV/AIDS depletes the human immune system, opening infected people to the ravages of opportunistic infections. That is, people do not die from AIDS, but from AIDS-related illnesses such as cancer and pneumonia. Everyone has heard by now how painful and devastating death from AIDS can be. It is a dreadful disease, indeed.

While HIV infection has appeared in every population, presently, certain populations continue at a higher risk for HIV infection than others do. People (men or women; gay/lesbian or heterosexual) who practice unprotected sex, particularly with multiple partners and/or IV drug users and their sex partners are most at risk for HIV infection. While powerful and effective medications for HIV treatment are available to some, many cannot access treatment because of poverty and/or lack of access to medical care. However, while there is no cure for HIV, because of the medical breakthroughs, most doctors and experts now consider HIV a chronic illness and not a guaranteed, short-term death sentence (Holt, Houg, & Romano, 1999). This is less true for HIV-positive individuals who are poor, without medical care, or living in poor countries around the world. For them, HIV infection means certain and painful death.

Beginning in the late 1980s and early 1990s, advocacy groups began fighting against inadequate resources for research and treatment, unjust social policy and public opinion, and a lack of passion and commitment toward the disease and the people infected with HIV. These groups have also fought to end discrimination and stigmatization that remains associated with HIV/AIDS. Over the years, the public considered people infected through blood transfusions more worthy of support than others were. Yet, these people still faced discrimination. For so long, HIV/AIDS has been a political and moral debate instead of an international health crisis. Even today, many people still believe that HIV/AIDS is God's way of ridding the world of "sinners."

Questions

As the author stated, HIV/AIDS is a pervasive problem affecting millions of people around the world. It is also an important issue for social work and all helping professionals, as it often devastates families and social networks. Yet, as much publicity as it has received over the years, it remains controversial among the public.

1. Explore the various, relevant literature to learn as much as possible about HIV/AIDS. Explore the history of the disease, specifics about the disease, its onset, routes of transmission, and medical and social treatments. Also, explore how HIV/AIDS has changed in recent years because of the new drugs available.

2. Further, explore public opinion about the disease and, more importantly, the people most believe get it (i.e., gay men). What barriers do these people face living with HIV/AIDS from the public, institutions, the workplace, and from medical and/or the social work profession? Discuss your findings with classmates, looking to learn their opinions about this disease, people who get it, and how the pubic and helping professions should treat people with HIV/AIDS.

3. Look into relevant policy considerations pertaining to HIV/AIDS. Based on your findings, what role do social workers play in shaping and/or changing public policy and/or public opinion?

4. Do a thorough and in-depth examination of your personal attitudes and beliefs about the subject. Locate the origin of your beliefs, and their potential

impact on how you would approach persons living with HIV/AIDS in personal and professional settings. Engage in a dialogue with classmates regarding this issue.

5. Examine issues pertaining to social class and current HIV/AIDS treatments. What can we do to help people receive lifesaving HIV "cocktails" who do not have the personal income or wealth to afford these drugs? Expand your exploration to the international level. Millions of people are dying of AIDS across the continent of Africa, for example. What policy initiatives could address this significant problem worldwide?

My Practice Environment

I worked with Bob and Phil in my role as social worker at a local clinic that specializes in the medical and social treatment of HIV/AIDS. Our clinic opened in the late 1980s, partly funded through Ryan White CARE act. The clinic also received funding from the state, local foundations, and a local private hospital. Every year, our funding was adequate for basic care, but never enough to provide the type of comprehensive services required by this population. Funding often relied on political goodwill. This was sometimes difficult to find because of attitudes and beliefs about gay men and the disease.

Medical personnel, infectious disease specialists, registered nurses, and a social worker (me) staffed the clinic. Additionally, the clinic provided community prevention and education along with housing services. We also relied heavily on local professional volunteers to provide services to our many clients and their families. The clinic was designed as a "one-stop shopping" venue for HIV-positive individuals and their loved ones. That is, we linked clients and loved ones to whatever service or support they required through the HIV/AIDS clinic. If the clinic did not provide a service, staff knew what organization did provide it and made sure that clients had access.

The environment served to normalize the diagnosis of HIV along with the many emotions, stigmas, and problems associated with this disease, especially in our local politically conservative climate. The clinic had approximately 400 HIV-positive clients at any one time; some had progressed to AIDS. Gay men comprised the majority of patients. It was not clear whether this represented the larger community or if non-gay, HIV-positive individuals went elsewhere for HIV services.

Client Engagement

I first met Bob during an emergency meeting at the clinic. One of our nurses came into my office and asked me to join an emergency meeting with a new patient and his partner. In my role at the clinic, I was used to these meetings. Someone was about to learn that they were diagnosed with HIV, and it was usually my job to tell them the news. I was responsible for crisis counseling, depending upon how the clients reacted to the devastating news. The day before, a doctor had hospitalized a local gay man for intolerable headaches. The hospital called in the clinic's infectious disease specialist to consult. They soon discovered that he was in late stage HIV. He had progressed to having AIDS. This is where I met Bob and Phil. Phil's headaches resulted from an opportunistic disease, a rare brain infection. It did not look good for him.

When I entered the examination room, Phil looked extremely sick. He was reclining on the examination table with his eyes closed. Bob was in the corner of the room, quietly crying. Our clinic doctor was talking to Phil about treatment options for pain, but neither he nor Bob were listening. Since the doctor was dealing with Phil, I moved across the room toward Bob. The doctor encouraged Bob to be tested immediately for HIV, since he and Phil were longtime sexual partners. I gently touched Bob's shoulder and asked him if he would like to come to my office for a drink of water. In shock, not really understanding what was happening; Bob leaned forward toward me, almost falling to the floor. I steadied his balance and led him to my office after telling Phil and the others that we would be back soon. I am not sure that Bob even saw me. He followed me down the hall to my office in a stuporous daze, as if he had just lost all of life's bearings. In fact, he had.

Bob sat down in my office. I used the time it took to get the drink of water to decide how to proceed, and to calm myself down. Even after several years of this work and numerous meetings where people learn their diagnoses, these moments do not become easier. Phil just learned that he would likely die; Bob learned that his longtime partner would likely die, and that he, too, might have HIV, if not AIDS. It doesn't get much "heavier" than that. It was clear that Bob and Phil were in crisis. While I did not witness the conversation and had not read the medical record, the diagnosis clearly caught both by surprise. They came in for a headache and left with an HIV/AIDS diagnosis.

I quietly reentered my office and offered the water to Bob. He held the cup and murmured, "Thanks." He looked dazed. I stood next to his chair and put my hand on his shoulder, hoping that he might find comfort through gentle, human touch. He needed to know that someone understood and cared. I quietly told Bob how sorry I felt about the out-of-control events happening around him. I wanted to be quiet and instill calm by decreasing the stimuli in Bob's environment. I told him that there was no rush for him to be tested and that when he was ready, I would do the test and the counseling myself. Bob began crying and asked, "Now what do I do?" He was not looking for answers; he was searching for something solid now that his once predicable life had spun madly out of control. At the most fundamental level, Bob had no idea what to do next—walk, breathe, sleep, cry, scream, or eat.

I excused myself to talk to the doctor and nurse to discover what they were planning. I went back into the examination room and listened to the end of the doctor's directions to the nurse and Phil. I told the doctor and Phil that Bob was in my office and that he would be back in a moment. Phil nodded his head indicating that he had heard me.

The nurse and I stepped out of the office and agreed to meet with Bob and Phil to review their immediate plan. Given their extreme level of anguish and shock, we agreed to discuss a plan for the next 24 hours only. Their crisis dictated that we not plan too far in advance. They would have enough trouble getting through this night. They agreed to meet their few friends, and contact others they knew with HIV to have a meeting at their house later that night. They were beginning to reach out for support. It helped that they knew others going through the same thing with HIV/AIDS. Yet, because of their recent move here, their network of friends and supportive people was small. After completing this meeting, we all scheduled an appointment to meet at Phil and Bob's home the next day.

Psychosocial Aspects of HIV/AIDS

HIV/AIDS brings with it many psychosocial issues needing attention by social work practitioners (Wright, 2000). Below, I discuss the issues I have seen most over the years, ones that practitioners must attend to during the period immediately following a new HIV diagnosis. I do not intend this as an inclusive list, only those issues that I believe are critical to address early in the process with clients.

Relationships and Intimacy

Other than mortality, an HIV/AIDS diagnosis involves and often changes the client's personal relationships. This is especially true for relationships with their parents, siblings, friends, and lovers. After diagnosis with this disease, little remains the same in their lives, or the lives of loved ones and friends.

Perhaps the most significant relationship changes occur in clients' future sexual contact with partners. Understandably, they fear rejection and worry about infecting others. This issue must be addressed early and often throughout work with HIV-positive clients. Mostly, it involves discussing client fears and educating them about their new and serious responsibility to protect others from infection. I recommend to clients that they either disclose when they first meet a potential lover, or wait to disclose when they decide that they would like a sexual relationship with the other person. Either way, I continually stress their legal, moral, and human mandate to disclose their condition to any potential or current sexual partner. Often, they will also ask about how to approach recent past lovers with this information. While health departments must locate partners for testing, I encourage clients to disclose to them first, to take personal responsibility whenever possible with friends and former lovers.

Relationships with family and friends can be more complicated. Many families still consider an HIV diagnosis embarrassing and shameful, even if their loved ones contracted it through blood transfusions. When the person is gay, it can carry even more embarrassment and emotional anguish. This is especially true if the client had not "come out" to their family and friends. In these cases, an HIV diagnosis makes everything public, and the resultant shock and anger can be as devastating as the diagnosis itself. I discuss this issue later in more detail.

Basic Needs

As in all crises, it is always important to deal with "first things first," especially during crisis periods. In other words, before spending time in more abstract pursuits such as feeling exploration, find out if clients have what they need to survive day-to-day. Clients will not discuss their feelings with honesty or meaning if they lack the basic resources to eat, sleep, and stay dry, out of the weather. Clients also need to consider transportation, medical access, and social support. Basic case- management skills are vital in helping clients to access financial support and helping programs. I also consider the emotional stability to survive the immediate crisis as a basic need. First, help clients make it to tomorrow, before worrying about the longer term.

Emotional Reaction and Stability

HIV/AIDS can be a lonely disease. Frequently, people keep their diagnosis a secret or tell only a small group of friends, family, or medical personnel. They rightly fear discrimination and stigmatization by the public, friends, and family. Because of negative public opinion, people living with HIV also risk losing their jobs or homes, as well as suffering verbal and/or physical abuse. It is important to remember that HIV remains a stigmatizing and socially isolating disease that frightens and polarizes most people. Not only do people live with a deadly disease, but they are sinners too.

Because their diagnosis is new and people often find themselves in emotional crises in the immediate aftermath, clients often ask, "How should I feel?" In fact, it is common to have clients grieving any loss ask the same question. They often feel so confused; clients asking this question simply want to know that they are normal, despite their confusion and constant emotional "flip-flops." I generally reassure clients that "normal" does not exist. Whatever they feel is normal for them, at that time. It also helps clients to know that others feel as confused as they do. Often, referral to a support group helps to ward off isolation and emotional crises, especially in newly diagnosed clients and their families.

Suicide

HIV/AIDS infected clients often present with suicidal thoughts, an important issue especially if your clients are gay or lesbian. Gay and lesbian clients attempt and commit suicide more frequently than heterosexuals (van Wormer, Wells, & Boes, 2000). My experience suggests that they become suicidal over their fear of pain and/or fear of dependency. Clients say that they do not fear death, but the process of dying. They do not want to face the pain and agony of death from AIDS, nor do they want to become dependent on others. They often lament the idea of their loved ones having to take care of them during late stage AIDS-related illnesses. Partners and caregivers often consider suicide because they do not believe they are up to the task of providing care, or do not want to live without their loved one.

In my experience, clients commonly stockpile medication so they can overdose if "things get too bad." However, clients in my practice rarely attempted or committed suicide. Medication stockpiles give them the comfort knowing that they "could" if they wanted to. These people feel so desperate and hopeless, that what they often need and want is someone to listen and gently educate them about life with HIV/AIDS. However, never take a suicide gesture or evidence of suicidal thought lightly. While most do not act, some will. Practitioners should evaluate clients to see if their suicidal tendencies are a normal reaction to their life, or caused by medications, psychosis, dementia, depression, or anxiety (Leavitt, 2000). If clients are serious, never hesitate to refer them to a psychiatrist for further evaluation.

Risk Prevention

As discussed earlier, an HIV diagnosis means that clients must immediately take responsibility for their sexual behavior or face legal consequences. Legally, HIV-positive people must inform sexual partners of their status or face serious legal consequences. Therefore, helping clients plan for sex and relationships is important, including frequent discussion of universal precautions and safe sex practices.

Dealing with Uncertainty

HIV/AIDS can be frustrating; there are no clear time lines or standard side effects. That is, the disease progresses differently in everyone. Clients want some predictability. They want to know what to expect, when to expect it, and specifically what they can do about the changes and problems when they occur. Hence, social workers must attend to their frustrations, as well as the plethora of questions clients have about their illness and what the future holds. Naturally, people want to know; they want a sense of control over their lives and future.

Moreover, many people base their expectations on the past, when HIV meant a shorter life. Many recall friends and acquaintances that died from AIDS. They are unaware of the way new antiretroviral medications have improved the quantity and quality of life for those with HIV. Hence, education is important to relieve anxiety and frustration.

Planning for the Future

Many HIV-positive clients lose the belief that their life has meaning. Victor Frankel (1959/1992) suggests that these crises of despair and distress highlight the need for meaning in life. Frankel views suffering as an opportunity for people living with a potentially terminal condition to grow and to learn ways to cope never before realized (Greenstein & Breitbart, 2000).

Our job is to help people look to their future with hope and planning. I routinely help clients plan for their future, set long-term goals, and not give up. I also help clients focus on their daily emotional goals, by encouraging them to live actively and engage with purpose and passion. Since we cannot make the "problem" disappear, providing a relationship based in hope is the most important thing a practitioner can do (Johnson, 2004) for a person newly diagnosed or the people who love a newly diagnosed person.

Handling the Crisis: Shock and Denial

One of my jobs as a social worker at the clinic is to inform clients about their HIV diagnosis. How people react varies, and is often determined by whether the client "knew" even before being tested. Some people come to the clinic having a sense that they have HIV, especially if they live a high-risk lifestyle. While news of the diagnosis is still painful and life-changing, these clients usually handle the revelation well.

If the diagnosis was a surprise, people often react with complete shock and emotional devastation; sometimes they lash out in anger or rage. In these circumstances, practitioners must continue reassuring them that help is available, and use crisis counseling skills to help clients process through this highly emotional period. Yet, do not expect clients to remember anything that you said, after the words, "You are HIV-positive." They will not remember anything, so keep your work simple and short term. In these circumstances, assess their immediate needs for support and protection, and try to contact them the next day to begin planning services.

Remember, similar to hearing about a loved one who died, everyone reacts differently to this news. Many are unprepared to accept the news or begin taking the steps to treat their condition. Most need time to process, either alone or with others. Moreover, denial is an important (and often healthy) coping mechanism for people newly diagnosed. Practitioners must remain patient, allowing this devastating news to "sink in" before demanding activities that require clients to accept their condition before acting. I always ask students to consider how long it would take them to adjust to the news. Never expect clients to act any sooner or differently than we would.

Questions

The author listed several psychosocial issues that she deems important from her practice experience. Yet, there are other factors to consider.

1. Explore the practice literature and best practice evidence to determine what additional issues are important considerations when meeting with newly diagnosed clients.

2. The author stated that few HIV-positive clients commit suicide. What does the professional literature say about this subject? What steps would ensure that clients do not harm themselves after diagnosis?

Our First Meeting

Before leaving for our appointment with Bob and Phil the next day, Katie (our nurse) and I agreed that we should focus on building relationships first. Katie said that she had several issues to review with Phil and that her only medical concern for Bob was his need to submit for HIV testing. We agreed that we would encourage Bob and Phil to develop a few manageable short-term goals.

We arrived at their home for our appointment. It was a beautiful new home in the suburbs. Bob was subdued when he greeted us at the door of their home. The inside of their home was as beautiful as the outside; clean, decorated, and warm. Bob took our coats and we approached Phil in the living room; Bob joined us. Phil was lying on the couch. We sat in the chairs facing the couch, Bob stood off to the side, refusing to sit.

I began the meeting by reintroducing Katie and introducing myself. I had not formally met Phil the day before. That is, we met but I was sure that he did not remember me at all. I explained our professional roles, discussed confidentiality, and had them sign the appropriate clinic forms and attachments. I expressed my sympathy for their emotional pain and offered our help to figure out their options. Almost immediately, Bob began crying. Phil's face did not move. He either was thinking, in heavy denial, or simply unable to process the issue at that moment. There we sat, Bob crying, Phil staring straight ahead, and Katie and I wondering what to do next.

Katie broke the spell by suggesting that we begin by reviewing our common understanding of the situation. This was our usual attempt to inform clients about the information we had and give them a chance to respond. Clients own the information in their medical file and it is important for them to know what information we had and our thoughts about their case. It is the best way to develop an open and trusting professional relationship.

Bob said that they were in the process of moving to this community when Phil began having reoccurring headaches, nausea, and losing weight. They had not lived here long enough to have many friends. Bob's company transferred him to this city two months earlier. They also did not have a doctor they trusted. The first doctor they met had difficulty determining a cause for Phil's condition. Frustrated, they met a different doctor who sent them to an infectious disease subspecialist, who made and confirmed Phil's diagnosis. Bob said that as gay men, they certainly knew about HIV, but had not considered that as an option. They had been together for many years and did not believe they were at-risk for HIV. Bob did say that Phil had recently confessed that during their estrangement, he had participated in anonymous sex. This was a new revelation that came out after Phil became ill and after they engaged in several years of unprotected sex.

Katie and I reviewed with them the facts about HIV. It is unwise to assume that people, even gay men, know about HIV transmission. Bob and Phil were surprised, as are most people, that a sexual relationship with Phil was not enough for Bob to contract HIV. Both Katie and I knew several long-time gay couples where one partner was HIV positive that regularly had unprotected anal sex. Yet, the other partner did not contract HIV. Most people do not know that conditions must be perfect for HIV transmission. That is, there must be an available route directly into the bloodstream for HIV to pass on. This is not always the case. I again offered Bob the opportunity for testing. After some thought, he agreed to the test, stating that he might as well know the facts. I suggested that early intervention was the best treatment.

Katie spent time talking with Phil about the medications and appointments that were needed for his care and treatment. Phil's affect remained flat and he did not reveal his emotions. He spoke very little, mostly with one-word answers. Phil seemed either overwhelmed, hostile, or perhaps he was experiencing some dementia because of his brain infection. I did not attempt to develop a relationship with Phil at this point, particularly since Bob seemed eager to have someone to talk to regularly. This time I asked Bob for a drink of water. While Katie wrote out directions and a timetable to review with Phil, Bob took me into their kitchen and gave me a brief tour of the house on the way. Bob and I sat at the kitchen table. I asked about his biggest worries at that moment. He was worried that Phil was going to die and that he would be alone in a strange city. He also worried that he would be unable to care for Phil and keep his job. He was also worried about the rocky relationships they already both had with their families, particularly with Phil's ex-wife and his adult children.

I was surprised that Bob never expressed concern that he might be HIV-positive. I finally asked him about it. He said that he didn't have time to worry about that now. He planned to take that news "as it comes." I supported his approach and his concerns. I asked if he could use help sorting through all that was on his mind and he jumped at the opportunity to see me while Phil participated in his medical examination the following week.

Bob's Personal History

While I did not know Bob's HIV status, he was the sole support of a man with AIDS, making him eligible for my counseling services at the clinic. He was in emotional distress and stating clearly that he needed to talk about his worries and fears. During our first session, with the help of information gathered during our home visit one week earlier, I learned about Bob's life and his relationship with Phil. He was forthcoming about his life and the struggles he faced as a gay man in a committed relationship and as the sole caregiver for a loved one recently diagnosed with AIDS and AIDS-related complications.

Presenting Problem

Bob stated that he presently had two physical problems. He reported an ulcer that he has been treating for four years and difficulty sleeping since Phil's diagnosis. He worried about how his lack of sleep interfered with his ability to work and care for

Phil, his life partner. Further, Bob said that he felt alone and overwhelmed by Phil's recent diagnosis of AIDS and the care he will require in the future. Bob did not believe that he had adequate social or emotional resources to cope alone with the pressures of life at this time. Bob's situation was more difficult because he and Phil had recently moved to the area, far away from family and friends.

As a gay man in a long-term sexual relationship with a man diagnosed with AIDS, Bob recognized that he was at high risk for HIV infection. While he stated that this concerned him, he was unable to devote much emotional energy to this possibility given all he had to worry about in his life. He stated that he would "cross that bridge" when he came to it after testing.

Bob sought help because his mind felt like it would "explode" and he had nobody to talk with in this area. Bob also said that he and Phil had not spoken since Phil's diagnosis. While Bob blamed some of Phil's reticence on his illness, he also believed that Phil felt guilty about not sharing the information about sex partners during their separations and protecting Bob during sex.

At the time of our first meeting, Bob did not believe he had the capacity to develop a plan of action and doubted that Phil, his partner, would be able to participate given his current medical crisis. Bob clearly expressed a desire for help getting through his current crisis.

Relationship History

Bob and Phil had lived together for ten years, having met at a nightclub in their former hometown. They had immediately fallen in love, and had worked hard to make a good life for themselves. As many young couples do, they had their "ups and downs" over the years. According to Bob, they had separated twice, once for one month and the second time for two weeks. Bob said that the issues that caused their separations were not serious, but the kind of "silly stuff" that all couples go through. It was during these separations that Phil engaged in unprotected, anonymous sex and contracted HIV/AIDS.

Presently, Bob was the sole caregiver for his partner. Phil was in the midst of a serious and complicated course of medical treatment for a rare brain infection. Bob said that he felt "numb" about the recent revelations about Phil's AIDS diagnosis and anonymous sex. He said that he did not have the emotional capacity to deal with the enormity of the situation, and did not know how to proceed as a primary caregiver to a person with Phil's serious medical complications.

Family History

Bob said that relationships with his family-of-origin were "complicated." Growing up, his family was lower middle class. While they had enough money to survive, the family struggled. He reported a good relationship with his parents and siblings growing up, but that changed when he met and moved in with Phil. Bob stated that his whole family struggled with his being gay and openly living with a gay man. It had taken several years before their relationships began improving. By the time he and Phil had moved to this area, he was again on "pretty good" terms with his parents and siblings, although they had not accepted Phil as part of the family.

Phil's family was more complicated. They not only had to deal with problems between Phil and his family-of-origin over being gay, but Phil also had an ex-wife and two adult children. Phil was older than Bob. As a young man, Phil had married a woman. They remained married for 12 years, raising two children. However, Phil finally realized that he could no longer stay in the closet and maintain his marriage. He divorced his wife and began living as an out, gay man. Within months, he met and fell in love with Bob. His ex-wife and two adult children never accepted his coming out. They remained angry with Phil and did not speak.

Bob stated that his family and support system of friends and loved ones lived several hours away. As stated earlier, they had recently moved to the community and had not been able to make many new friends before Phil's health deteriorated. He expressed gratitude that he and his partner had moved into their home. However, their move was recent and he did not feel settled or grounded in his new home or community.

Professional Career

Bob stated that he worked hard and earned a generous salary. He was worried what would happen at work when Phil needed care at home. Bob was unsure how his company would respond because he had not revealed that he was gay at work. According to Bob, it was not that he considered himself "closeted" at work; he simply had not told anyone. Since his company did not recognize domestic partners as spouses, he did not believe he would qualify for leave to care for Phil.

Bob did not drink or use drugs other than an over-the-counter sleep aid. He again reported that he slept poorly since Phil's illness and that his work was suffering. He was afraid that his job performance was "slipping" and that he was losing his short-term memory.

Client Strengths

Bob was intelligent and well socialized. He had a good job, nice home, food, and adequate financial resources. He appeared concerned about Phil, despite an underlying sense of betrayal. Although he was emotionally hurt, he knew that Phil was critically ill and needed his help. Bob was not used to asking for help and was eager to begin problem solving. He recognized that his issues were unfamiliar and was grateful to have found helpful community resources.

Questions

Now that the author has presented information about Bob's life, and before reading on, perform the following exercises based on your education, experience, the professional literature, and best practice evidence. To increase the learning potential of this exercise, you may want to do this in a small group with other students in your course.

1. Based on the information in this case, construct a three-generation genogram and eco-map that represent Bob's personal, familial, and environmental circumstances. What further information do you need to complete this exercise? What patterns do these two important graphical assessment tools demonstrate?

2. Write a complete list of Bob's issues and strengths, focusing on Bob's multi-systemic environment.

3. Write a two- to three-page narrative assessment that encompasses Bob's multi-systemic issues and strengths. Review Chapter 1 if needed. This narrative should provide a comprehensive and multi-systemic explanation of his life as he prepares for therapy with the author.

4. Try to identify the theoretical model or approach that you used to guide your assessment. According to the literature, what other theoretical options are available and how would these change the nature of your assessment?

5. The author did not provide a clinical diagnosis. However, as a student you should take every opportunity to practice this process. Therefore, develop multi-axial DSM-IV-TR diagnoses for Bob based on the information provided above and in your assessment narrative. Be sure to look for evidence of multiple diagnoses on Axis I. Provide the list of client symptoms that you used to justify your diagnostic decisions. What, if any, information were you missing that would make this an easier task?

6. Explore the practice literature to find what approaches are best suited for working with clients with Bob's issues and strengths. What special issues would ensure proper treatment that encompasses the various issues in Bob's life?

7. Develop a treatment plan, complete with goals and objectives, based on Bob's unique circumstances, your narrative assessment, diagnoses, and the practice literature. Compare your treatment recommendations to other's in your class and seek to understand any differences that arise.

Treatment Planning

Based on the information gathered during our meetings, Bob and I developed a treatment plan that addressed his most important issues. His plan included, in his own words, the following goals, and objectives.

Goal 1: Bob states that he wants improved sleep.

Objectives:

Seek assistance from physician.

Develop a self-care plan that includes proper diet and regular meals.

Develop a self-care plan that includes delegating some of his work and worry to others.

Goal 2: Bob states that he wants to develop a social support network.

Objectives:

Keep counseling appointments with the HIV counselor.

Connect with the emotional support of friends from home.

Attend a church in the area accepting of gay members.

Contact the Lesbian and Gay Network in the community to receive a newsletter and make social connections.

Goal 3: Bob is concerned about his high risk for HIV.

Objectives:

Set an appointment for HIV testing and counseling at the clinic.

Use universal precautions in caring for his partner.

Consistently engage in protected sex to reduce chance of infection or re-infection.

Questions

1. Compare the treatment plan you established above with the author's treatment plan. What differences and similarities exist between the plans? How do you account for the differences? Use the professional literature and practice evidence to analyze both plans, and the differences between them.

2. Develop a revised treatment plan from information provided by the author, your original plan, and the practice literature. What does the evidenced-based practice literature say are the most effective ways to treat clients with Bob's problems and strengths? Using the rationale from the literature and your experience, develop a position on this issue.

Ethical Challenge with HIV-Positive Clients

Perhaps the most significant issue for people with HIV is confidentiality. A person with HIV is at-risk of overt and covert discrimination. People living with

HIV also risk losing relationships and social support systems once people know they are HIV-positive. This important issue should be handled delicately and with care.

Social workers should not second-guess clients about whom they can safely tell and who they cannot. For example, a young man I once treated told me that he was worried about telling his mother about his HIV. I was tempted to think about my supportive relationship with my own mother and believe that a mother is a vital person to include in care. Just because I would trust and include my mother does not mean that this client should do the same with his mother. We make a big mistake when we push clients to share information based on our assessment of their support group. Ethically, we interfere with their right to self-determination and breech their right to confidentiality by using our professional relationship to encourage them to tell someone about their status. I encourage newly diagnosed clients to resist telling too many people, too quickly. I suggest that they take time to allow their own shock to wear off before assessing who needs to know and who will offer support and encouragement.

Questions

The author just presented an interesting ethical challenge that arises when clients learn that they have HIV/AIDS. That is, the issue of "coming out" about their illness is serious and must be carefully considered by clients. The same issue is important when treating gay and/or lesbian clients with or without HIV/AIDS. Since every practitioner will ultimately work with gay and lesbian clients, whether they realize it or not, it is important to grasp the complexities of this issue before confronting it in practice.

1. Explore the professional literature pertaining to working with gay, lesbian, bisexual, or transgendered clients. What does it recommend about the issue of coming out? What best practice approaches are available to guide practice decisions with this important issue?

2. Explore your personal beliefs and attitudes about gay, lesbian, bisexual, and transgendered clients, as well as people infected with the HIV/AIDS virus. As you prepare a position on working with these populations, examine how your personal beliefs and attitudes shape and/or affect your professional position on this issue.

3. Explore the professional code of ethics to find the relevant standards that apply to this issue in practice. What are your professional obligations pertaining to HIV/AIDS, coming out, and your role in the process?

4. It might be helpful and instructive to discuss this issue with student-colleagues to discover their findings and personal beliefs regarding this critically important practice issue.

Intervention Plan and Course of Treatment

The treatment plan served as a vital platform for my work with Bob. When we first met, Bob's life overwhelmed him, rendering him unable to take action on his own behalf. Given Bob's personal style that required organization and a plan of action, writing a treatment plan might help him take action.

Our first activity was to list Bob's most significant worries. I served as his scribe in this exercise. Once the list was complete, I asked which of his worries were priorities and in what order (based on priority) would he rank them? For example, Bob listed Phil's health problems, but through our discussion, I learned that Bob was relieved with Phil's new doctor and nurse involved in his case. He was impressed with their care and attention, as well as their willingness to include Bob in decision making. Thus, Bob agreed that this worry could move down the list since Phil was being well cared for by the medical staff at the clinic. The process of sorting through Bob's worries was helpful for motivating Bob into action. This process took two one-hour sessions to complete. When he finished, Bob decided that his top priorities included his lack of sleep, lack of social support, HIV testing worries, and the need for a plan of action, the issues that ended up on his treatment plan above. Bob was pleased with our work and placed a copy of the plan at home to keep him from feeling besieged and overwhelmed.

Biopsychosocial Model

I utilized the biopsychosocial model to approach Bob in our early sessions. This model seeks to reconcile the combination of body, emotions, and social integration by treating these human components as collectively maintaining the function of the whole (Engel, 1980). This model further suggests that all levels of human organization interact and that change in one area of functioning affects change in another (Caron & Goetz, 1998). This derivation of systems theory asserts that any treatment of an individual must take into account not only biological disease but also emotional states and social support. In work with HIV related clients, the biopsychosocial model offers three distinct areas to work on with the understanding that progress in any area means progress in all areas. Hence, I shared with Bob that his life was not as compartmentalized as believed. I promoted the idea that his health, emotional and physical self-care, and social support all played an important part in his survival. We discussed how all aspects work together to promote his overall health and well-being. Bob responded well to this approach, and seemed to be making progress. However, his life was about to change again.

HIV Testing and the Results

One week after we met, I tested Bob for HIV. Bob was HIV-positive. While he knew that the possibility existed, Bob had not thought about his own health status because of everything else that was occurring in his life at the time, especially Phil's deteriorating health. The news was a blow to Bob. He struggled with feelings of anger toward Phil for "giving him HIV" and his concern about Phil's rapidly declining health. Again, he found himself feeling unable to move. He was sick, and his future was as uncertain as Phil's was. However, the changes were not over.

About one month later, Phil died of his brain infection, an AIDS-related complication. Bob was devastated. It was stunning to consider how many earth-shattering events had befallen Bob in such a short time. His life revolved around the security of a long-term partner that he loved, their two good jobs, two good incomes, and both in good health. Three months earlier, their life was optimistic and full of opportunity. Within three months, Bob was planning Phil's funeral, having problems at work, and learned he was HIV-positive. It was a credit to Bob's strength of character that he endured under the pressure.

Ongoing Therapy

Following Phil's death, Bob and I met once per week for approximately six months. Over time, we scaled back our meetings to once per month, and then once every six months as he progressed and improved his life. We built our counseling relationship around his needs as they presented themselves.

We spent the first few months after Phil died talking about his anger at Phil for dying and infecting him with HIV. Bob realized that Phil had known he was sick for a while before telling him. This left Bob wondering why Phil, the man he loved, would put him at such risk. He could not justify Phil's inability to tell him, or insist on safe sex after their last separation. This issue would haunt Bob for a long time. His sense of betrayal was keen, and he had great difficulty forgiving Phil for "ruining" his life in a reckless and thoughtless manner.

Bob also worked hard to understand his role in his family-of-origin. He knew that his family considered him the "gay son." Before Phil's diagnosis, their relationships had improved. However, since his HIV diagnosis and Phil's death, Bob's relationship with his family deteriorated. His family told Bob that he "deserved" HIV for being gay. Obviously, he did not receive support from anyone in his family-of-origin.

Then, Bob's life changed again. About six months after Phil's death, Bob's HIV became full-blown AIDS. Bob was frightened, certain that he was going to die soon. He immediately took steps to receive long-term disability from his job and continued to take care of himself by working out, and eating and sleeping well. He began seeing our medical team for what treatment was available at the time. It looked as if his life had taken its last drastic and cruel turn.

Yet, despite the changes he underwent inside one year, Bob began making connections in his new community. He linked with a local church and the local Gay and Lesbian Network. He developed a close-knit group of supportive friends and soon found himself feeling emotionally better than he could ever remember. I was amazed by his commitment to life and his ability to make the best of his difficult circumstances.

Questions

1. Take a moment to review Bob's progress in treatment. Based on the author's description, the professional literature, and the latest practice evidence, what occurred to account for his progress?

2. What was the theoretical approach or combination of approaches that appeared to work best for Bob?

3. Based on the work you have done earlier, what additional intervention(s) would you recommend for Bob? Use the literature and latest practice evidence to justify your recommendations.

Termination

Finally, Bob's life took a turn for the better, in an amazing way. Soon after his HIV became AIDS, the new antiretroviral medications came onto the market, and Bob could afford them. These amazing drugs saved Bob's life. He made steady progress until he was able to return to work and live a full and healthy life. After seeing Bob off and on for five years, he had moved on in his life. He had new friends and new life's purpose. He no longer needed me as a support in his life; he received what he needed from his new community. When we last met, Bob was living a full life, working full time, and enjoying the company of good friends.

It seems ironic to say that Bob was lucky. His diagnosis occurred shortly before the new antiretroviral medications became available. These medications prolonged his life. Not only has Bob now lived with AIDS for 8 years, he remains strong and vital and has a good quality of life. While I have not seen Bob professionally for a couple of years, I continue to see him at local events and fund-raisers and we greet each other joyously.

Questions

The author presented an interesting, successfully terminated case that involved many issues commonly found in medical social work practice with clients living with HIV/AIDS. Taking a broad view of this case, reevaluate the author's work and your participation through the questions asked throughout the case.

1. Overall, what is your professional opinion of the work performed in this case? As always, refer to the professional literature, practice evidence, your experience, and the experience of student-colleagues when developing your opinion.

2. Based on this review, what additional or alternative approaches could she have used with this case? That is, if you were the practitioner, how would you have approached this case? Please explain and justify your approach.

3. What did this case demonstrate that you could use in other practice settings? List the most important things you learned and how you could apply these lessons in your practice career.

Bibliography

Averitt, D. (2000). HIV/AIDS and social work: The medical context. In V. Lynch (ed.), *HIV/AIDS at year 2000: A sourcebook for social workers*. Boston: Allyn and Bacon.

Caron, W., & Goetz, D. (1998). A biopsychosocial perspective on behavior problems in Alzheimer's disease. *Geriatrics, 53*(1), 56–60.

Engel, G. (1980). The clinical application of the biopsychosocial model. *American Journal of Psychiatry, 137*(5), 535–544.

Frankel, V. E. (1959/1992). *Man's search for meaning* (4th ed.). Boston: Beacon Press.

Greenstein, M., & Breitbart, W. (2000). Cancer and the experience of meaning: A group psychotherapy program for people with cancer. *American Journal of Psychotherapy, 54*(4), 486–500.

Holt, J., Houg, B., & Romano, J. (1999). Spiritual wellness for clients with HIV/AIDS: Review of counseling issues. *Journal of Counseling and Development, 77*(2), 160–170.

Johnson, J. L. (2004). *Fundamentals of substance abuse practice*. Pacific Grove, CA: Brooks/Cole.

Leavitt, E. (2000). Mental health issues in HIV disease. In V. Lynch (ed.), *HIV/AIDS at year 2000: A sourcebook for social workers*. Boston: Allyn and Bacon.

van Wormer, K., Wells, J., & Boes, M. (2000). *Social work with lesbians, gays, and bisexuals: A strengths perspective*. Boston: Allyn and Bacon.

Wright, E. (2000). The psychosocial context. In V. Lynch (ed.), *HIV/AIDS at year 2000: A sourcebook for social workers*. Boston: Allyn and Bacon.

3

Stephanie and Rose Doer

Rose Malinowski

Introduction

The following case demonstrates another of the different problems that hospital social workers encounter during the course of a typical day. Here, social worker Rae Miller meets Stephanie, a teenage mother about to give birth to a newborn with a serious disability. Stephanie's mother, Rose, while being supportive of her daughter, had no idea that Stephanie was pregnant before doctors announced she was about to go into labor. In this case, Rae Miller guides this family through a difficult period, and difficult decisions regarding the new baby, child care, medical care, and parent training. She also helps the family navigate the various systems that poor families must confront after giving birth to a baby with significant disabilities.

The Doer Family

It was a typical Wednesday afternoon when hospital social worker Rae Miller received a page calling her to the labor and delivery suite. Rae Miller worked in the high-risk pregnancy and the neonatal intensive care units at Unity Medical Center. Responding to the page, Rae met Sarah, a nurse caring for a 16-year-old mother-to-be in labor. Sarah and Rae had worked together many times supporting young mothers through the labor and delivery process, helping them to make plans for themselves and their newborns. She had no specific reason to believe that this case would be any different from others, but Rae had learned to expect the unexpected.

The Presenting Problem

"We have another teen mom who's had no prenatal care. She's hardly in labor and is already screaming in pain," Sarah said.

Stephanie, the 16-year-old African American young women now in labor, had arrived at the hospital emergency room two hours earlier. Her mother, Mrs. Rose Doer, accompanied her to the hospital. Stephanie had stayed home from high school that day complaining that she felt nauseous and tired. Mrs. Doer came home at lunch to find Stephanie in severe pain. She rushed her daughter immediately to the hospital. Though it was farther from their home than another hospital, Mrs. Doer knew her daughter would receive the care she needed at Unity. Mrs. Doer was distraught. Stephanie was her only daughter and she was definitely in medical crisis. She had no idea what was wrong with her daughter, and Stephanie was not talking.

Unity Medical Center

Unity Medical Center is a large medical facility in a major midwestern city with over 500 patient beds and many specialty clinics. Specializing in neonatal social work, in the areas where Rae worked, she encountered women on a daily basis with pregnancy complications including diabetes, hypertension, and substance abuse. In the neonatal intensive care unit, Rae helped families struggling with the reality of sick and developmentally disabled newborns. Many times these newborns were born prematurely with a variety of special medical and developmental needs. Some were full-term babies needing major surgery while others were born with congenital anomalies. Rae enjoyed the opportunities and challenges she faced in her job. She also enjoyed working at a hospital with an excellent reputation in the community.

Hospital Social Work

Before returning to Stephanie and Rose, it is important to discuss the field of practice known as hospital social work. Social work practice in a hospital setting offers unique challenges in a fast-paced environment. It provides social workers like Rae the chance to interact simultaneously with many different clients interacting with multiple systems using various methods of treatment. One of the biggest challenges involves balancing social work responsibilities with clients and their families with the multi-systemic hospital environment. That is, they must help clients navigate the complexities of laws and policies, medical personnel, length of stay limitations, funding, and discharge planning. This requires social workers to work well under pressure, and in a rapid and timely manner to help clients and the hospital meet their goals.

Hospital social workers routinely interact with regulations from the federal government, legal system, and third-party insurers; hospital policy and local healthcare organizations and institutions; and the stresses and issues presented by patients and their families as they grapple with their personal circumstances. To be effective, practice demands brief intervention combined with short-term case management and personal training and education, an understanding of relevant laws and policies, and familiarity with funding and managed care providers.

Often, social workers only see patients and/or family members once or twice before they discharge. Therefore, the time line for performing an assessment, developing a treatment plan, and implementing this plan with the cooperation of the patient and family is shorter than in many other practice settings. Hospital social workers must learn to engage people rapidly for an assessment and discharge plan. Their primary function is to provide patients and families with emotional support while helping them move through the health system, from admission through discharge.

Hospital social workers contribute to patient care as a member of a team of professionals. Their goal is to complete a psychosocial assessment, deal with any existing emotional needs during treatment, as well as design and implement a safe and appropriate discharge plan in an environment of limited resources. These days, financial considerations play an important role in most healthcare decisions. Medicare, Medicaid, private insurers, and HMOs (health maintenance organizations) greatly influence the utilization of services for their enrollees.

Cost Containment and Managed Care

Because of the emphasis on cost containment, social workers work closely with the utilization review (UR) team to ensure a safe and timely discharge within the guidelines of the patient's funding source. The role and function of UR is to make recommendations about the need and appropriateness of continued hospitalization for individual patients. The impact of UR is primarily financial: when the committee determines that a patient's medical condition no longer warrants hospitalization, a third-party payer frequently discontinues payment for inpatient care.

This applies significant pressure on healthcare teams to meet a patient's medical, emotional, and discharge needs in a timely manner and, hopefully, under budget. Hence, hospitals work diligently to monitor length of stay and to discharge patients when acute care services are no longer necessary. Because insurers can deny or stop payment, hospital personnel closely monitor patient length of stay and discharge patients once their medical condition requires a less costly environment. Whereas in previous eras, patients were often given extra time in the hospital to ensure recovery, today that is not the case. Patients discharge immediately after becoming stable enough to leave.

Questions

Similar to all areas of practice, managed care and organized cost containment measures greatly affect how hospitals provide services. As the author stated, as

soon as patients are medically stable and able to move, they are discharged home or to a lower-cost, less intensive placement. Many in social work and health care believe that managed care has weakened the system and placed patients and their families at risk. Others believe that managed care makes efficient use of limited resources to provide care for the greatest number of people possible. Nonetheless, this remains a hot topic across the healthcare delivery system.

1. Examine the professional literature regarding managed care and its affect on healthcare delivery, including social work services. During this investigation, be sure to explore any outcome studies that compare treatments in and out of managed care environments. Write a critical essay, demonstrating the findings from the literature that ends with you taking a definitive position about the value of managed care in healthcare and social service delivery systems.

2. Examine the code of ethics (NASW, 2000) to determine how social workers should approach issues that arise because of managed care. Present all sides of your arguments and attempt to develop a process for using the code of ethics to evaluate treatment and discharge decisions.

3. Engage with classmates in a dialogue about this topic. Managed care and client funding will be a significant part of professional practice. Listen intently for the different opinions and beliefs about the impact of managed care on the profession.

In addition to the financial emphasis, the social worker ensures that patients and their families do not become lost or overwhelmed in the intimidating hospital environment. Working from a systems perspective, hospital social workers attempt to restore a patient's dignity during this stressful and vulnerable time. Social workers are the first line of defense against patient and family alienation and intimidation, representing the humanistic element of the healthcare system. Social workers listen to patient stories, learn about their fears, recognize their part of a complex system, support them through the hospitalization, and ease their transition back home or onto their next level of care.

Using a strengths-based approach (Saleebey, 1997) is the most effective approach in a hospital's fast-paced environment. A strengths-based approach focuses on client resources and strengths in their multi-systemic environment to help patients meet their goals. The hospital environment does not allow time to focus too long on client problems or deficits. Patients must be empowered to take charge of their situations and make decisions in a short time period. For example, with the Doers, Rae Miller worked to organize family support networks, provide parent training about child care generally and training to meet the specific needs of their newborn, and engage other healthcare organizations to give the family the best chance for success after discharge. Empowering patients and families to be self-sufficient is an important component of helping with personal adjustment after a medical issue or crisis.

The process of helping patients and families recognize and utilize their strengths to help meet their needs is empowering. Commonly, the technology of medicine, the medical jargon, or fear of the unknown involving their illness intimidates patients and their families. This often leads to feelings of isolation and vulnerability at a critical time when patients need comfort and reassurance. Hospital social workers try to help patients overcome their fears.

Hospital social workers also help patients transition back into the community. Although it can be a frightening and traumatic experience coming to the hospital, it can be even more frightening to leave. Hospital social workers address the emotional issues that result from the stress and change after hospitalization. Their job is to listen, validate, encourage, teach, empower, and apply professional use of "self" to affect lives. It is important for social workers to rely on "self" to be effective in any practice setting.

Arriving at the Emergency Room

When they arrived, Mrs. Doer escorted Stephanie through the hospital doors as she doubled over in pain. Mrs. Doer called for medical help. A security guard quickly assisted Stephanie to a wheelchair, and wheeled her to the front of the line at the registration desk. Mrs. Doer struggled to get her insurance card out of her purse, attend to Stephanie, and tell the registration clerk her name, address, and phone number. Stephanie began quietly crying for someone to help her. She was in a lot of pain.

"It hurts so bad, mama," cried Stephanie.

Mrs. Doer gathered her courage and demanded help for her daughter. "My daughter is in so much pain. I don't know what it is. She was fine yesterday and now look at her. . . . Please help her. . . . She needs a doctor," Mrs. Doer pleaded.

The reception clerk explained that all of the examination rooms were full, but a doctor would see Stephanie as soon as possible. A long twenty minutes later, medical staff ushered her into an examination room. The doctor asked Mrs. Doer to wait outside while he examined Stephanie. A short time later, the emergency room doctor emerged from the room to meet with Mrs. Doer.

"Stephanie is in active labor and is being transported to the labor and delivery suite. I need to ask you about your daughter's medical history so that we can help her," the physician said. Almost in shock, Mrs. Doer told the doctor that her child was a normal, healthy teenager. "Stephanie goes for a physical every year and is fine. She has no allergies and no heart trouble. She hardly misses a day of school." . . . Then it hit her, "She's pregnant . . . How can that be, I mean . . . how can my baby be nine months pregnant and I didn't know it. Look at her, she's so thin. She can't be pregnant." Obviously, Mrs. Doer did not know that Stephanie was pregnant. Rae had seen cases before where the expectant mother had managed to keep her pregnancy a secret. However, it usually happened in disconnected families. That is, girls and/or women can easily hide a pregnancy when nobody pays attention to them. The Doer family was different. If anything, their family was enmeshed, making this even more difficult for Mrs. Doer to understand, and accept.

Regardless of the family situation, there were other potentially troubling aspects of this case. Rae wondered what steps Stephanie undertook to conceal her pregnancy. Usually, women trying to conceal their pregnancy forgo prenatal care and proper nutrition. That is, they nearly starve themselves and their babies trying to avoid gaining weight. Perhaps, they continue smoking, drinking, or using drugs as a way of distracting people around them from realizing that they are pregnant. While Rae did not yet know if this was the case with Stephanie, she worried that the baby might have problems caused by poor prenatal care and, especially, lack of proper nutrition.

Labor and Delivery

Rae Miller received a verbal report of Stephanie's admission history from Sarah. This was Stephanie's first pregnancy. Nurses reported that the vital signs were good for both mother and baby. On examination, the baby appeared to be nearly full term. The ultrasound technician verified the child's size and attempted to determine if the infant had any apparent abnormalities. Rae decided this would be a good time to meet with Stephanie and her mom, before the labor contractions became too frequent and too intense for them to talk.

The first meeting is the most important facet of developing a working relationship with patients, especially with such a young mother. She was frightened about her pain, having a baby, and because her mother just discovered that she was pregnant. This was a lot for a 16-year-old to process while simultaneously enduring significant pain. Once the baby is born, Rae knew that Stephanie would have so many needs. Rae would have to let her know that they will tackle her needs together. Once the labor pains started to come more frequently, Stephanie would be completely focused on her body and delivering this baby. Rae decided that the best time to talk to Stephanie was before she went deeper into labor.

Questions

The client, Stephanie, presented at the hospital as a pregnant teenager. Her mom appeared to be surprised to learn that Stephanie was pregnant. This is a prescription for problems. Imagine you were the social worker assigned this case and answer the following questions before moving ahead with this case.

1. What is your first hunch regarding this case? Explore the practice literature and discuss this issue with other students to identify any relevant issues that you should consider with the Doer Family.

2. What is the next direction of inquiry and assessment? Further, explore the practice literature to locate theories or models that apply to this type of work. Based on the approaches you find, what information would you need to

collect to perform a comprehensive and/or multi-systemic assessment? (See Chapter 1).

3. What personal strengths can you locate and name at this early juncture in treatment?

4. As you prepare to proceed with the Doers, what issues or concerns do you have pertaining to Stephanie's pregnancy, given that her mother did not seem to know that she was pregnant? Use the literature and dialogue with classmates to add to your thought process.

Rae Miller

After finishing her MSW field practicum at River Valley Health Center, Rae knew she wanted to work in a medical setting. The fast pace and rich learning environment appealed to her. Now in her second year at Unity Medical Center, Rae enjoyed working in an environment that provided her with various opportunities and challenges including supporting families through difficult transitions, learning about new technologies developed to help mothers and infants, and working with a team of healthcare professionals.

Rae approached her job with enthusiasm and an open mind. She came from a family where caring for each other and sticking together through difficult times was important. She remembered the time her father was in the final stages of Parkinson's disease, her brothers and sisters joined together to provide the physical and emotional support he and the family needed. Raising children with love and providing a solid education for them was a primary focus in her family.

Rae carried these life experiences, her enthusiasm, and compassion for children with her as a professional social worker. She approached Stephanie's room with a sense of confidence that she could help this new family discover their potential for tackling the unexpected birth of a child. Rae had never worked with teenagers before coming to work at Unity. Since she had been there, teenagers had taught her a lot about hope and endurance. While many believe that teenagers rarely tell the truth, Rae discovered that it was important to listen to them, to hear what they had to say. When practitioners have the skill to develop trusting relationships with teenagers, they can provide unique and important insight about themselves, their world, and those around them.

Questions

Rae was assigned a case that involved an African American single-parent family, where a 16-year-old girl was about to have a baby out of wedlock. Given the nature of this case, their needs, Rae's background and belief system, and potential cultural issues and factors pertaining to the Doer family, please respond to the following questions as if you were the social worker responsible for this case.

1. **What cultural, racial, or ethnic issues are apparent in this case? Explore the professional literature on cultural competence and health care to determine the issues that you should watch for when trying to engage Stephanie and Mrs. Doer.**

2. **Based on the results of your literature search, your personal and/or professional experience, and through critical dialogue with classmates, what approach would you take with this family to demonstrate cultural competency in your work?**

3. **Based on the information you obtained above, what particular issues relevant to African American families and adolescent mothers are important to address in this case scenario?**

Developmental Milestones

Since she began at Unity, Rae had gained firsthand knowledge about the adolescent struggle for identity. Rae frequently encouraged teenagers to explore questions about themselves and their future lives. For example, she helped teens answer questions such as "Who am I?" "What do I want out of life?" "Will I finish school?" "Will we marry each other?" and "Where will I live with my new baby?" Rae explored their self-image, peer relationships, and family support as a regular part of her assessment with teens. She was interested in learning how teenagers learned to make independent decisions and how their families helped them explore their emerging personal values and make plans for the future. Especially with teenage moms, Rae discovered a common link between body image and self-image. Often, she met young mothers who were putting themselves and their babies at physical risk by not eating properly or adequately. These mothers often felt pressured to maintain a "thin" physical appearance like the majority of their peers, despite being pregnant.

Questions

1. **Based on the information you have to this point, make a list of the issues that you are most concerned about, those that you want to address during your early meetings with Stephanie and her mother. What issues does the professional literature suggest are important to include in an assessment with a teenage girl about to give birth?**

2. **Also, at this point identify any strengths she may have in her multisystemic environment.**

First Meeting with the Doers

Rae entered the room armed with her knowledge, experience, and enthusiasm. The small room was full of monitoring equipment for the mother and baby. "Hello, my name is Rae Miller and I am the social worker for the moms and babies unit. I'm here to help you with any questions you may have," Rae said to Mrs. Doer and Stephanie.

Rae realized that she was fortunate to meet Stephanie and her mother during a time when activity was at a lull in this crowded room, full of noisy equipment and medical personnel coming and going. Sometimes it seemed so hectic and chaotic that Rae found it difficult to believe people actually knew what was happening. Yet, everyone received the proper care. She thrived on the hectic and fast-paced environment of the hospital. It certainly kept her day interesting. From all appearances, Rae knew that she would only have a few minutes with them, as Stephanie's labor was progressing. Rae at least wanted to introduce herself as a helping person and let them know how they could reach her.

Although she did not expect to have much time for conversation, Rae understood that she could learn a lot about the family from observing them together in this stressful time. Rae was pleasantly surprised to see Mrs. Doer doing her best to support her daughter through the delivery. Mrs. Doer stood by Stephanie's bed with a cloth to wipe the sweat from her face and provide a supporting hand on Stephanie's arm.

Countless times, Rae had seen teenagers alone and scared as they brought a new life into the world. Rae had seen many families, locked in their shame and anger, turn away from young women in similar situations. Instead of experiencing joy of anticipated childbirth, she usually met families struggling over keeping the pregnancy secret, their fears about the potential loss of their daughter's future goals and happiness, and/or their anger at either their daughter, the father of the child, or themselves as parents. Today was different. Stephanie appeared safe and supported with her mother. As Rae approached Stephanie's bedside, Mrs. Doer reached to shake her hand.

"Thank you for coming," Mrs. Doer responded quietly, "I just want my daughter to be okay."

Stephanie was almost mute during Rae's first visit. She looked at Rae and then closed her eyes. Then, her face contorted as another contraction began. Rae stepped to the side so that Sarah, the nurse, could help Stephanie ease the pain. "I'll be back to talk to you both soon," Rae told them. She knew that this was a bad time. Stephanie and her mother had bigger concerns than talking to a well-wishing social worker. They had a baby to deliver.

As Rae walked away, she wondered what questions and needs this African American family would have, and hoped she could help them. Mrs. Doer's openness and support of her daughter was encouraging, yet Rae knew that many unknowns lay ahead. Rae wondered what emotional and financial supports the family had and what psychological resources they possessed to help them deal with the shock and stress of an unexpected newborn. She also wondered how the secrecy of the pregnancy would play out in the family as time passed and the crisis subsided. Rae knew that Sarah, their nurse, understood and worked well with the uncertainties and fears that teens present during this intense period. Thankfully, the mother and baby appeared healthy.

Medical Crisis

Rae remained on the hospital floor charting her first contact with the family when the attending physician pulled her aside.

"Stephanie is about to deliver a baby with anencephaly," the doctor told Rae. "Come with me to the delivery room. They may fall apart when I tell them."

Rae was in shock herself. A little while ago, everyone seemed healthy and happy. Now, Stephanie's baby would be born without all or most of a brain. Between contractions, the doctor explained this serious medical condition to the mother and grandmother.

"Stephanie, the ultrasound showed us that your baby is a boy. It also showed an abnormality in the baby. He will be born with a condition named anencephaly. There is no easy way to say this. The baby will be born without all or most of a brain. Babies who are born with this condition do not live long; usually they die shortly after birth. Do you understand, Stephanie?" the physician asked.

"No," Stephanie yelled, "No!"

"Nothing can be done to prevent this, Stephanie. A major portion of the brain did not develop. He may be able to breathe on his own for a while, but he will not be able to see, hear, or eat because his brain is not there to help him. The baby's face and the rest of his body developed normally, but his skull is ill-formed. The skin on his head covers an abnormally shaped skull. I know this is not the news you expected to hear," the doctor went on to explain, "but you needed to know this as soon as possible."

Stephanie's eyes welled up with tears. This was almost too much to process, on what was becoming a miserable day in the Doer family.

"Can't you help my grandson?" Mrs. Doer questioned.

"No cure exists for this condition, ma'am. The medical team is here to support you through this very difficult time," the doctor replied.

"Would you like me to call anyone for you?" Rae asked.

Mrs. Doer replied, "No, there isn't anyone who can help us with this."

Before she left for the day, Rae alerted the hospital chaplain and social worker on call about the Doers and their potential crisis. The family told her that they were Roman Catholic, and Rae thought they might benefit from the comforting presence of a priest. She also left the on-call social worker a brief summary of the immediate situation, including the family's potential need for grief counseling and information about funeral planning. Rae went home that night feeling sad for the family. How difficult; a young mother would have to say goodbye to her baby so shortly after it was born. Sometimes, life is cruel.

Questions

This turn of events calls into question many ethical issues pertaining to the birth and the medical care that will be required. Moreover, it further suggests that the family might have to make significant life-or-death decisions about their baby. As the social worker in this case, explore the professional literature,

especially related to the ethical implications of this scenario to learn about the various options and choices that this family may face. Based on what you learned in your literature review, answer the following questions.

1. As a teenage mother, what rights does Stephanie have when making grave decisions about her baby's medical care? Do her rights change if these decisions specifically involve life-or-death decisions such as removing life support? How do her age and the gravity of the baby's condition influence this situation?

2. What ethical, legal, and client cultural considerations must be addressed concerning the possibility of abortion and children conceived with anencephaly? What are the laws in your state concerning abortion, this specific medical condition, and the mother's age?

3. Explore the professional literature to determine the issues related to the psychological and/or emotional stress and trauma families experience that choose abortion versus deciding to give birth to children with this serious medical condition? During this review, please account for your political and/or religious beliefs about abortion and how they might influence your decision-making process.

4. Based on your findings and your knowledge of professional social work practice, what responsibilities do you have as the social worker in this case?

Stephanie's Baby

Through Stephanie's tears and pain, the medical team delivered her newborn baby boy later that night. John Doer was born with a full head of curly black hair and shining brown eyes. He was a beautiful baby, weighing close to four pounds. At first glance, he appeared normal. However, under the newborn's soft hair, his skull was flat. John made no sound, and did not move on his own. He was breathing, a good sign. Doctors quickly gave John to Stephanie, wrapped in a blanket with a small cap on his head. They wanted her to hold him before he died. She smiled at him and held him tight. The priest arrived and baptized John at the family's request. Everyone believed he was about to expire. Surprisingly, John had a different idea. Four hours after his birth, and long after doctors thought he would die, John continued to breathe on his own.

The Following Morning

As Rae drove into work, she anticipated a message from the on-call social worker saying that Stephanie's baby had died overnight and updating her about any funeral arrangements to follow up on that day. No such message arrived. Perhaps the on-call social worker forgot, or would tell her in person.

As she did everyday, the first thing Rae did in the morning was attend medical rounds in the neonatal intensive care unit. As the team made rounds, they came to John's bed. Rae saw John for the first time. He was a handsome child. Doctors confirmed during the night that John was anencephalic, but his curly hair covered the malformation of his skull. From looking at his sweet face lying so expressionless in his crib, Rae could not tell there was anything wrong with him. In this case, John's looks were deceiving.

Healthcare Team Meeting

During rounds, the healthcare team of physicians, nurses, Rae, chaplain, and physical therapist met to discuss the immediate plan of care for John and to decide how to approach the family. The big question the team needed to answer was whether to provide him nutritional support now that he was breathing independently. During the meeting, and much to her dismay, Rae detected prejudices against African American teenage moms in the tone and content of the team's discussion. While this angered her, she was glad that these issues surfaced at the team meeting rather than in front of the family. She had to speak on behalf of the family. Being her client's advocate with the healthcare team was a major part of her job.

"It is important to involve Mrs. Doer in the decision making due to the gravity of the situation and Stephanie's young age," Rae began. "Yes, this young mother has the legal right to make healthcare decisions for John. None of us knows how long John will live. It is crucial for us to support this family as they grieve the loss of a healthy baby; deal with the turmoil caused by an unexpected delivery, and plan for an uncertain future."

"Sarah, the nurse who took care of them in labor and delivery, reports that Stephanie appears shy, but she cooperated during the delivery. The grandmother works full time, and was in the delivery room to help her daughter through the process."

"At least this is one family not living on the welfare dole," the attending physician stated. "I know what you're going to say, Rae, each family is unique and has their own strengths and needs," he said, "but you must admit that most black families in these circumstances seem to end up on welfare."

"Well, this family is different, and most African American families do not end up on welfare, it only seems that way to you. Have patience Dr. _____ , I wonder what this family will teach us," Rae responded.

Rae felt frustrated with the medical team and their attitude. She hoped that her face did not show it. As she sat there in disbelief at their overtly racist comments, Rae was remembering how much time she spent educating the medical staff about effective communication with families from different cultures. She wondered if they would ever understand.

As a social worker, Rae valued the uniqueness of individuals and the importance of upholding their dignity and worth. She took seriously the need to practice in a culturally competent and informed manner at all times. At patient care conferences, Rae often discussed cultural issues and their relationship to the plan of care. The team talked about how the family's beliefs, values, and religion affected health-care decisions, the influence of gender roles in child care, involvement of the extended family in providing emotional and material support, and many other cultural issues. During these team meetings, Rae thought that the staff was receptive and thought the discussions were helpful. Yet, when it came to speaking about specific family situations, individual team members' biases frequently surfaced. Rae thanked her social work training for the knowledge and increased self-awareness about cultural differences, and for the opportunities she had to play the role of a social work educator.

Questions

1. Earlier, we discussed cultural competence as it applied to the social worker role in this case. Here, we learned about potential problems with others on the healthcare team responsible for Stephanie and John's medical treatment. Based on what you discovered earlier and your knowledge of social work roles and responsibilities, what is your obligation pertaining to cultural competence with the healthcare team?

2. Evaluate the approach Rae used with the doctor that made the insensitive statement in the meeting described above. When you are in this position (and you will be, if you haven't already been), how would you handle a similar scenario? If you have already been in this position, what did you do to intervene?

Family Meeting

Rae, the primary nurse, and the attending neonatologist entered Stephanie's room to discuss the immediate option of feeding John. Rae was relieved to see Mrs. Doer was in the room. She was clearly fatigued, but her appearance was still as neat as the day before. Stephanie looked at the medical team with fear in her eyes, anticipating that John had died. Instead, the attending physician reviewed the facts of John's current medical condition.

"Stephanie . . . John has done well in the last few hours. His vital signs are good and his respiratory status is stable," the physician began. "Now we need to decide if we will give John tube feedings so that he will get the nutrition he needs to survive. Since he cannot swallow on his own, with your permission we will place a tube in John's nose right down to his stomach so that the food will go straight there. Without the feedings, John will die in a few days."

The nurse showed Stephanie and Mrs. Doer the tube and how it would feed John.

"Stephanie, none of us knows how long John will be with us. We do know that if John survives he will need care around the clock for the rest of his life. He may also need another medical procedure, a shunt, which would help to manage the flow of cerebral fluid in John's body since he does not have a brain to help with this. He does not need this now, but he may in the next few months. Otherwise, his head will continue to swell as it fills with fluid. We need to make a decision about feeding John soon. What do you think?"

"I can't let my baby starve," Stephanie responded. "His eyes are so bright. . . . I know he's looking at me and I can't let him down." Stephanie looked at her mom and they both agreed; John was alive and he needed their help.

That Afternoon

After the meeting, Rae's work began in earnest. The baby had survived, at least for a while. The family decided to give him nutritional support to prolong his life. Soon, doctors would discharge Stephanie from the hospital. Hence, Rae needed to quickly assess the family's situation and help them develop a plan of action. Although John's future was uncertain, it was important for the family to explore alternatives for his care.

Along with the nursing team, Rae encouraged the family to hold John, as well as bathe, feed, and exercise him. This was the first step in bonding with John and helped Stephanie begin learning about his special needs. Rae knew how important it was to engage the family in John's care before they left the hospital and returned to their daily lives. He would need extensive follow-up care, including medical appointments and physical therapy. She knew from experience that families did not bond successfully with their child unless they developed a partnership with the healthcare team around the care of the infant within the first few days following birth.

Family History

Rae spoke with John's primary nurse about the family. She knew a little more about the family than Rae did. No one had yet been by to visit or call about the baby, suggesting that Mrs. Doer and Stephanie lacked outside support. The medical record revealed that Rae's mom worked as a secretary in downtown Detroit. Stephanie was an only child, a sophomore in high school. She had not listed the name of the baby's father or any other emergency contacts.

Then, Rae saw Mrs. Doer walking down the hallway toward the nursery as she was leaving. "Would you like to see your grandson, Mrs. Doer?" asked Rae.

Mrs. Doer responded with a hesitant look. Rae escorted her into the nursery to John's bedside. "He has a tube in his nose, but he looks okay. I don't understand. I don't understand how he can breathe without a brain. He must have a brain," Mrs. Doer began.

The nurse asked, "Mrs. Doer would you like to hold him?"

Almost as if she was unaware of where she was, Mrs. Doer said, "Stephanie is a good girl, passing all her classes. We go to church every Sunday. I work hard to provide for my daughter. What will I do now?"

She was afraid to hold her new grandson. Perhaps she was not ready yet. Only a few hours earlier, Mrs. Doer did not even know that Stephanie was pregnant. Now, she had a grandson with special needs, clinging to life through a feeding tube. It is little wonder that she hesitated. John was the embodiment of everything in her life that had changed forever. However, Mrs. Doer seemed like a loving and supportive woman, Rae was sure that she would come around . . . in time.

The Grieving Process

Thus began the process of acknowledging John's presence in her family and the grief surrounding his birth. Mrs. Doer wept while holding John. This was not the grandchild she had dreamed of, nor was this the ideal time. She had high hopes that Stephanie would graduate from high school and marry before having a child. Mrs. Doer felt as if she had lost her daughter, too.

Rae intervened, "It's okay to cry. All types of feelings are normal at a time like this. Suddenly Stephanie has a baby with special medical needs. This is a lot for anyone to handle. What's important now is for you and Stephanie to spend time with John and work with the medical team to plan for his care."

After a few moments of fighting back her tears, Mrs. Doer said, "Stephanie needs to visit John and learn to care for him. We don't know when we'll have to say goodbye to him and he is such a beautiful child. Stephanie's a little afraid." With that, Rae left to give Mrs. Doer time alone with her new grandson.

Engaging Stephanie

Rae proceeded down the hallway to meet with Stephanie. She brought along a picture of John. Stephanie stared at the picture, avoiding Rae's eyes. Rae informed Stephanie that John was being fed and that she could visit him anytime.

"How are you feeling today, Stephanie?" Rae asked.

Stephanie remained silent.

"It can be a confusing time with so many feelings and thoughts running through your head," Rae stated. "Stephanie, you need to know that whatever you decide to share with me is private information. I will not share what we talk about with anyone else unless I talk to you first."

"How are you feeling, Stephanie?" Rae asked again.

"I'm scared. I hid the pregnancy from my mom and everyone else. I tried not to eat much so I wouldn't show, and I didn't brag about it at school like the other girls do. I didn't know the baby was coming so soon! This wasn't supposed to happen. I wasn't supposed to get pregnant before I was married. Now what do I do?" Stephanie went on to talk about how disappointed her mom must be and how Mrs. Doer had always insisted that Stephanie marry before having children.

"Your mom is here helping you now, Stephanie. Who else can help you? What can you tell me about the baby's father?" Rae asked.

"He's in my school too. He knows I was pregnant. I'll call him and tell him about the baby," she said.

Rae realized that this young girl was struggling with being an adult and a child simultaneously. Stephanie did not want Rae's help communicating with the baby's father. She also said that she did not want to talk anymore about him. She wanted to keep his identity a secret. It would be the father's choice to come forward or not. From her experience, Rae realized that many teenage mothers were hesitant to reveal any information about their baby's father for fear of the father's reaction. They also want as much control as they can have during their stressful time. It is always important to involve fathers in the process of planning for their child's future, unless the mother refuses to allow it to happen. Rae always worked to encourage their participation.

Questions

Confidentiality is a major part of the code of ethics (NASW, 2000). This issue can become uncertain when it pertains to confidentiality between adolescent and other family members.

1. What issues arise related to confidentiality when speaking to Stephanie? As the practitioner, what obligations do you have in revealing information obtained from Stephanie to her mother? At 16 years old, does Stephanie have the right to confidentiality?

2. How does the scenario differ, if at all, when speaking to Mrs. Doer? Are confidentiality requirements the same or different between mother and daughter?

3. Explore the literature to discover how confidentiality rules and regulations pertain to Rae's ability to communicate with other members of the healthcare team.

Over the next couple of days, Rae gathered more information about the family during interviews with Stephanie and Mrs. Doer. Rose Doer divorced her husband 10 years earlier because of his drinking. She did not know where he was now. Mrs. Doer and Stephanie lived in a two-bedroom apartment. Mrs. Doer's annual income was $26,000. She and Stephanie were close. They mostly kept to themselves. They both attended Saint Rose's church in their neighborhood, but were not involved with any church activities.

Stephanie liked some of the teachers at school and had a few friends. After school, she usually went straight home because their neighborhood was rough and the gangs at school had "control" of the neighborhood. She liked to read and listen to jazz with her mother. Neither Stephanie nor Rose mentioned any extended family or friends at church or in the neighborhood that could help them. Obviously, the Doers had little social support. Mrs. Doer said that she was hesitant to reach out to anyone in the neighborhood because gang and drug activity were so intense. She did not know whom she could trust. She also said that she was too tired after work to go to church beyond attending Mass on Sunday.

Discharge Planning

The time was approaching for Stephanie to leave the hospital. Because of his condition and medical needs, John would have to remain in the hospital for some time. As Rae met with Stephanie to plan her discharge, she said, "John will always need someone to be with him and help him. Our medical team has talked about what John needs and that he can only stay at the hospital for a short time to receive this kind of care," Rae explained. "After that, you will perform this at home, or in some other fashion in the community."

As Rae and Stephanie spoke, Mrs. Doer entered the room. "I don't know what to do with him, he's so sick. I want to finish school, and mom has to work. What will we do?" Stephanie asked.

Questions

Johns has serious, long-term medical needs, and the hospital will not be able to provide this care onsite for very long. His long-term care will be expensive and time consuming, and the Doer family is busy, while living on $26,000 per year. While Mrs. Doer's health coverage paid for Stephanie's delivery, it is likely that it will not cover the baby after Stephanie leaves the hospital.

Based on the information gathered and presented above about the family and John's condition,

1. What financial and social supports are available in you own state for children who have special medical needs and for their families?

2. What is your role as social worker in locating these benefits for your client?

Locating Help in the Community

In addition to dealing with the emotional trauma of sick newborns, Rae frequently helped families locate financial support to care for their children. Over the years, Rae had become an expert on social security disability benefits, Medicaid, specialized state programs for children with special medical needs, and had spoken to many private insurance carriers to determine what supports they offered for families with sick babies. Rae's expertise really helped many families. At times such as these, families need facts to make long-term care decisions and support in working through the maze of services.

Rae explained the situation to the Doers. "Stephanie and Mrs. Doer, John is eligible for financial assistance because of his disability through the social security office, and for medical insurance through the public aid department. Mrs. Doer, your medical insurance will not cover John after Stephanie leaves the hospital. The billing office here at the hospital will help Stephanie apply for medical insurance that will pay for the rest of John's stay at the hospital and for his care when he leaves. I can help you apply for disability income."

"At least that's some help," Mrs. Doer said with a sigh of relief.

Stephanie looked at us both with a glazed look in her eyes. She was struggling to understand all this information. Rae was relieved to have Mrs. Doer present during this time.

"Do you have any questions, Stephanie?" Rae asked.

"Not now," Stephanie answered. "I just want to go and see my baby."

"Great!" Rae said. "I'll stop by later for a visit."

Rae observed Stephanie sitting by John's bedside, watching the nurse change his feeding tube. The nurse in the intensive care unit explained to Stephanie and her mom that she was John's primary nurse. "I'll be in charge of caring for John while he's here and teaching you how to care for him too. I know you'll be going home soon, Stephanie, but we'll be here to show you and your mom how to change John's feeding tube and all the other things you'll need to know to take care of him. We can train anyone else you choose to help out too," the nurse told Stephanie.

"When John goes home, a nurse from home care services will come to your apartment for a short time to support you and continue teaching. They will follow up on the physical therapy program we will show you here to prevent John's limbs from stiffening and contracting. These exercises will make it easier for you to care for John as he grows. You will also be trained to look for the signs and symptoms of cerebral fluid build-up in John's head," the nurse said.

Mrs. Doer practiced John's physical therapy routine, moving John's arms and legs for him under the supervision of his nurse. Stephanie remained glued to her chair.

Finally, Mrs. Doer told Stephanie, "Hold him. He's your baby."

Stephanie quietly obliged and began to stroke her baby. Throughout that day, Rae observed Stephanie's shock and denial at her son's birth and affliction. Stephanie seemed to want nothing more than to turn back the clock and return to the familiar routine of school, reading, and jazz. Rae wondered how this family could possibly care for John at home. He needed nurturing and care around the clock. Additionally, he could die at any moment. Though John's brain stem now supported his breathing, he could still stop breathing at any time. Since he could not move, John was at high risk for pneumonia and bedsores, despite being so young.

The home care nurse would visit the Doer home the same day John returned home and prepare them for these potential problems as well as provide them with education and support. Rae knew that it was always different for families when they must care for their baby at home. They are alone. The nurses are not there to help or answer their questions. As you might expect, families are afraid they might do something wrong. The stress of constant care of a sick or disabled infant begins affecting most families almost immediately after discharge.

John presented different challenges than most babies. When he needed care or was distressed, John would not cry or fret as other sick babies. Moreover, the Doers would also learn that John could not respond to their touch, eye contact, or voices as other normally developing babies do. This might be the most difficult part of all. While most parents marvel at their baby's development related to touch and communication, the Doers would not have the chance to experience these joys. Because of his disability, John was unresponsive.

Once John discharged, the hospital team would see John and Stephanie on an outpatient basis. As part of the planning for John's discharge, the family would return for regular medical appointments at the high-risk clinic. At this clinic, all the healthcare specialists from the neonatal intensive care unit would continue to monitor John's overall health, respiratory, and neurological status.

Rae would offer family counseling to support them through the grief and adjustment period. The emotional and financial burden of caring for a baby like John would be tremendous for any family, and Rae worried about this family. They had so few resources and a teenage daughter with so many needs herself. She chose to work with the family as a unit because of Stephanie's current fragile emotional state and her mother's apparent open, supportive attitude toward both her daughter and grandson.

Providing New Alternatives

Before the end of the workday, Rae informed the Doers that they had another option for John's care. "I understand you'll be going home tomorrow, Stephanie, and I wanted to give you some other information before you left the hospital. In Detroit, there are a few nursing homes that take care of babies like John," Rae shared.

Rae gave them this information because Mrs. Doer needed to return to work and Stephanie wanted to finish high school. They certainly did not have to make the decision immediately, but Rae believed that they needed to know the option existed.

"These pediatric nursing homes would welcome a visit so you could see the facility and ask questions. These homes are specially licensed to care for children with serious medical needs like John and their staff is trained to care for children. This may be an alternative for John's care now or at a later date," Rae told them.

Stephanie said, "I want to take him home with me." Mrs. Doer agreed.

Rae thanked Stephanie and Mrs. Doer for helping so much that day, reminding them that she understood how much information they had to digest. She also reiterated that she and the healthcare team were there to support them. The information the family provided would help the team do this. Rae encouraged Mrs. Doer to go home and for both to get some rest that night. Rae said goodbye and said that she looked forward to visiting with them the next day.

Later That Night in the Nursery: Meeting John's Father

Stephanie and her boyfriend, Tyrone, visited John that night. Tyrone was proud of his son. Tyrone was 17 years old and a junior in high school. He was not a good student, but attended school regularly and had not joined a gang. Tyrone challenged Stephanie and the nursing staff regarding the health of his son.

"He looks normal. He'll learn how to eat and run someday. You've got to be wrong," Tyrone stated.

Both Tyrone and Stephanie held John a long time that night.

Questions

Now that the author has presented information about the Doer family's life, perform the following exercises based on your education, experience, the professional literature, and best practice evidence. To increase the learning potential of this exercise, you may want to do this in a small group with other students in your course.

1. Construct a three-generation genogram and eco-map that represents the Doer family's personal, familial, and environmental circumstances. What further information do you need to complete this exercise? What patterns do these two important graphical assessment tools demonstrate?

2. Write a complete list of their issues and strengths, focusing on their multi-systemic environment.

3. To assist with the next step, consider the following issues in your investigation:

    A. What are the salient developmental issues confronting the Doer family and the infant's father, Tyrone?
      1. What is the nature of John's developmental delays?
      2. How did the pregnancy and John's medical condition potentially affect Stephanie's development?
      3. What developmental tasks was Mrs. Doer struggling with in her life?
      4. What developmental tasks was Tyrone struggling with in his life?

    B. What grief issues did the family face because of the birth of a physically handicapped child?
      1. What will they face if John lives? What if he died?
      2. How would their issue be similar or different during a medical crisis with an adult versus an infant?
      3. Does the type of medical crisis influence the grieving process? Explain how and why.
      4. In your state and/or locale, what resources are available to families grieving the loss of a child?
      5. What support services are available to those families who have a child diagnosed with anencephaly during pregnancy? What about after the baby was born?
      6. What support and information would you find important to provide for families who become aware of this congenital anomaly during pregnancy? What about after the baby was born?

4. Write a two- to three-page narrative assessment that encompasses the Doer's multi-systemic issues and strengths. Review Chapter 1 if needed. This narrative should provide a comprehensive and multi-systemic explanation of their life as they prepare to leave the hospital.

Stephanie's Discharge Day

Rae arrived at work and immediately checked to see if Stephanie was going home as planned that day. She needed to contact Stephanie before she left to question her about her immediate plans and her thoughts about caring for John. Rae had contacted Stephanie's high school to set up a home study program for her during the six-week postnatal period. Stephanie began working out plans to visit John once she was home. Rae checked with the nursery to discover that John had a good night and that both parents had visited with him. Rae was elated at this change of attitude. Stephanie successfully fed John and changed his diaper. The father held him. John's parents were beginning the bonding process.

Stephanie went home that afternoon, while John remained in the hospital. The nursing staff told her that they would monitor John's weight and respiratory status. He now weighed four pounds and could leave the hospital after gaining one more pound. Stephanie shared that she was optimistic John would continue to do well. "I can tell by that sparkle in his eyes," she said.

Rae met with Stephanie that day and learned that John's father, Tyrone, would drive her to the hospital to visit John. Her mother was busy buying a few things for the baby, and would be in that afternoon to take Stephanie home. Rae let Stephanie know she would be checking in with her the following Monday.

Stephanie went home that day feeling supported by her mom and Tyrone. This positive beginning encouraged Rae. She believed that they (including the healthcare staff) had done all they could do to establish an open, working relationship with the family. They had encouraged the family to spend time with John, provided them with information about his needs and available supports, and begun training them to care for John.

The First Few Weeks

Stephanie returned to the hospital the following week to visit John. Rae was unable to meet with her as Stephanie mostly visited in the evening with her mother. John slowly gained weight. His neurological and respiratory status remained stable. The nursing staff was encouraged that both Stephanie and her mother participated in John's care, held him, and talked to him.

Rae called the Doer's home the Monday after Stephanie's discharge and spoke with Stephanie. The first and subsequent telephone conversations with Stephanie were short and factual. "I'm fine," Stephanie said, "Just waiting for my mom to come home so we can visit John."

Rae asked if Tyrone had been visiting the hospital. "No, but I'm okay. My mom drives me," Stephanie answered in a mechanical, flat tone of voice.

Rae wondered if Stephanie was slipping into a depression. Sadness was a normal part of the grieving process. With John as sick as he was and without daily routine and supportive contacts with Stephanie, the risk of clinical depression for her was even higher. Telephone follow-up conversations with this family did not appear to be enough. Rae arranged to leave a note for the family with the nursing staff asking Stephanie and Mrs. Doer to schedule an evening appointment with her.

Tuesday Evenings

Over the next three weeks, Rae met with Mrs. Doer and Stephanie four times for evening appointments in the intensive care nursery. Tyrone had not returned to see John.

When she asked about him, Stephanie reported, "Tyrone's busy at school and he's on the basketball team." She obviously did not want to talk about him.

Mrs. Doer reported that Stephanie was eating and sleeping fine, and that she did not seem bothered by John or Tyrone's absence. Stephanie appeared most animated when interacting with John. She smiled brightly and caressed him gently. "He's my bright eyes . . . and he's getting so big," Stephanie said.

However, Mrs. Doer began showing signs of stress. She was having trouble sleeping and complained of headaches. "I want Stephanie to finish school, but I know she's not studying at home. I don't see a way out. I visited the nursing homes you told me about, but Stephanie won't even talk about it," Mrs. Doer stated.

"He's coming home, mom. I told you I'll take care of him," Stephanie retorted. "He'll be fine."

Stephanie remained adamant about staying home and caring for her baby. She did not verbalize any concerns or ask questions about John's future, except those directly related to his day-to-day care. Mrs. Doer continued to hope Stephanie would at least get her GED.

Rae knew that presenting both in-home and out-of-home options was important for all families. Her social work training had taught her that families needed adequate information to make their own decisions. The Doers were eligible for Medicaid and specialized home care services because of John's medical condition and their low income. Home health care would provide respite services, nursing, and therapy services, but would not provide 24-hour care. Rae took special care in explaining this to the Doers, along with information about 24-hour care available in pediatric nursing homes. They needed to decide what they wanted to do about John. Rae had done everything she was capable of doing on their behalf.

Going Home

John had remained in the hospital for three more weeks after Stephanie went home. He slowly gained weight and his respiratory status remained stable. His accumulation of cerebral fluid was minimal. Stephanie learned all of John's routines and had the proper formula, written instructions, phone numbers, and pictures of the medical staff with Stephanie and John the day she took John home.

Rae arranged to be there for John's discharge. She encouraged the family to return for their follow-up visits in the high-risk clinic. At the clinic, the neonatologist would assess John's overall health while the neurologist would monitor the need for a shunt. Stephanie stated that she did not need to meet with Rae after discharge. "I know how to take care of John. My mother can talk to you if she wants," Stephanie said. "I'll ask the doctors for what I need." Mrs. Doer did want to meet with Rae. She arranged late afternoon appointments so that she would not have to miss work.

The day after discharge, a home healthcare nurse called the intensive care nursery with a routine report about the admission visit for the Doer family. The nurse observed Stephanie feeding John and doing his physical therapy routine, as scheduled. John's vital signs and neurological status remained stable. The home was clean and well kept. Stephanie appeared to be caring for John very well. The nurse would return to assess Stephanie's ability to change John's tubing and monitor his neurological status. She would review with Stephanie the steps she would need to take if John started to run a fever, spit up his food, or showed signs of difficulty breathing. The nurse anticipated that she would visit the Doer home one to two times per week for the next month to reinforce the education and training begun in the hospital. She would report again as discharge from home care services approached.

Over the next month, Stephanie brought John to the hospital clinic twice. John's condition remained stable and Stephanie continued to care for him while her mother worked. Stephanie chose not to participate in any meetings with Rae, saying that she was doing fine on her own. Rae had received good reports from the home care nurse about Stephanie's involvement with John and so she did not insist that Stephanie participate in any additional counseling.

Questions

1. **Stephanie decided against aftercare services with Rae. Given her age and rights as John's mother, do you have any concerns about Stephanie at this time?**

2. **If so, what course of action would you take to address these concerns, and how do you square your decisions with the ethical standard related to a client's right to self-determination?**

3. **Do Stephanie's age and the seriousness of John's condition affect this important ethical standard?**

4. **How are the ethical values of dignity and worth upheld by your opinion and proposed approach to this case?**

Outpatient Counseling with Mrs. Doer

Mrs. Doer opted to attend weekly individual counseling sessions with Rae. "I want Stephanie to come in with me, but she's stubborn. I'm scared for her and for John. What will happen to them?" Mrs. Doer asked.

With Mrs. Doer, Rae focused on issues related to the family's adjustment to having John at home and the resultant stresses for Mrs. Doer. By this time, John was over a month old and though gaining weight, he could not move on his own or react to the world around him, including his family. "Stephanie's not facing it. He's not getting better," Mrs. Doer said.

Rae worked with Mrs. Doer, helping her to identify her fears for John and Stephanie. After a time, Mrs. Doer finally faced the issue that John could die at home and neither she nor Stephanie was prepared for this.

"I've lost so many people in my life. I'm afraid I'm going to lose both of them," Mrs. Doer revealed. "Both my parents died when I was young. My aunt gave me a place to live and food to eat. When I was nineteen, I married and moved to Detroit with my husband. He had trouble finding regular work and started drinking. One day he didn't come home. Finally, I divorced him and I haven't seen him since. Now John could die and I could lose him too."

Mrs. Doer talked about her belief that she had failed Stephanie, just as she failed her husband. "I found a job as a filing clerk at the same company I work at now. If I had spent more time with my husband, maybe we'd still be together today," Mrs. Doer said. "I know if I'd spent more time with Stephanie, she wouldn't have gotten pregnant. John's a punishment for my failure as a mother."

Rae worked with Mrs. Doer for the next two months, acknowledging her feelings of guilt and reframing her perceived failures as tangible ways Mrs. Doer was helping John and Stephanie now. In addition to dealing with the possibility of John's death, Rae also guided Mrs. Doer in examining some long-term decisions that the family may face as John grew and continued needing care.

Saying Goodbye

Stephanie did not return to the high-risk clinic. However, she moved John's care to a pediatrician closer to her home. This change in John's follow-up medical care meant that Rae could no longer meet with Mrs. Doer for counseling at the hospital clinic.

Because she was preparing for termination, Rae reviewed with Mrs. Doer the gains she had made in her counseling sessions. Mrs. Doer could articulate her fears and anxieties concerning the futures of John and Stephanie, as well as some realistic goals for them.

"I know Stephanie is a smart girl and she'll go back to school someday," Mrs. Doer said. "John . . . I just want him to be loved and not to suffer."

Mrs. Doer developed coping mechanisms for herself. She became active in a support group for families with special needs children. Mrs. Doer decided not to rush home every day from work at lunchtime to check on her daughter and grandson. "I need some time for myself too," she realized.

The home care nurse had stopped visiting the Doer home one month after John went home from the hospital. The nurse's assessment found the infant to be medically stable and the family to be independent in their care of John.

Rae confirmed with Mrs. Doer that the financial applications for social security disability income and a medical card for John were complete. "Stephanie should begin receiving disability payments for John within the next month," Rae explained. Mrs. Doer said that this helped to relieve her stress and that she believed that she could manage on her own now. Mrs. Doer chose not to continue with individual counseling services at a different agency.

While writing her closing notes, Rae felt sad and optimistic for the Doers. Both Stephanie and her mom had shown positive signs of coping. Stephanie had remained at home, bonded well with John, and was taking good care of him. Mrs. Doer had gained many insights about the crises she faced and was using these insights to cope with the challenges she and her daughter faced everyday with John. Still, John's prognosis was poor with every moment an uncertainty. She wondered how the family would fare in the future. It was an open question. Rae was satisfied that she did all that she could do to prepare them for the future. Now, it was up to Stephanie.

Epilogue

Five years later Rae Miller was teaching a class of foster parents at a local community college about special needs children in foster care. As the class ended, a young woman entered the room to pick up a friend attending the class.

She walked up to Rae and asked her, "Do you remember me? I'm John's mom."

Rae received a special gift that night. Stephanie showed her pictures of John at five years of age. After about six months of caring for John at home, Stephanie had placed him in a nursing home.

"They love him there, too, and I visit him all the time. He's a miracle. He needed that shunt and he made it through the surgery. He still has those beautiful bright eyes," Stephanie talked through a grin of a proud mother.

Rae remembered, too, the gleam in those beautiful brown eyes.

Questions

The author presented an interesting case involved many issues commonly found in medical social work practice. Taking a broad view of this case, reevaluate the author's work and your participation through the questions asked throughout the case.

1. Overall, what is your professional opinion of the work performed in this case? As always, refer to the professional literature, practice evidence, your experience, and the experience of student-colleagues when developing your opinion.

2. Based on this review, what additional or alternative approaches could the author have used with this case? That is, if you were the practitioner, how would you have approached this case? Please explain and justify your approach.

3. What did this case demonstrate that you could use in other practice settings. List the most important things you learned and how you could apply these lessons in your practice career.

Bibliography ―――――――――――――――――――――――――――――

National Association of Social Workers. (2000). *Code of Ethics of the National Association of Social Workers.* Washington, DC: Author.

Saleebey, D. (Ed.). (1997). *The strengths perspective in social work practice* (2nd ed.). New York: Longman.

4

Annie

Joan M. Borst

Introduction

I met Annie while working as a social worker in a community healthcare clinic. The clinic provided healthcare services to homeless individuals and families. I met Annie one morning while walking through the neighborhood. I had never seen her around before. She was young and pretty, with an edge that said, "Don't mess with me." I wondered how a young women like Annie ended up living on the streets. While I did not yet know her, I was sure that, similar to other homeless women, Annie faced many barriers in life that prevented her from reaching her personal goals. From my experience, I knew that she was probably at risk for many problems, including substance abuse, HIV/AIDS, unplanned pregnancy, physical or sexual abuse, along with a plethora of health-related problems.

I first noticed Annie during morning rounds (see below), and immediately recognized her as new to the community. When I stopped to greet a small group of familiar faces, I said hello to Annie, and she responded with a big, toothy smile and a look of naïveté that concerned me. I always wondered how these young women survived each night, given the threats present on the streets and in the mission. I encouraged Annie to drop by and "check out" the services at the healthcare clinic anytime she wanted. I asked the others to tell her about the clinic and give her directions.

Homeless women encounter many forms of discrimination and alienation. They are cut off from mainstream support, particularly vulnerable to physical and sexual abuse, and have a lower life expectancy than other women have. Homeless women are also prone to disease, particularly sexually transmitted diseases, such as syphilis, HIV, and chlamydia. It is even worse for homeless women of color.

They are particularly vulnerable because of their experience with racism. Moreover, these women usually end up at the bottom of the waiting list for available services and are the least likely to apply for social services (Kushel, Vittinghoff, & Haas, 2001).

Like so many others in the homeless community, Annie represented several different cultures. She was African American, young (19 years old) and attractive, born to a troubled family in a poor rural community two hours north of the city. She was homeless, developmentally disabled, and possibly mentally ill. While she appeared tough, she was vulnerable. I heard through the local "grapevine" that several men routinely took advantage of her both physically and sexually since she moved into the neighborhood two weeks earlier. Annie became homeless when her family forced her out of their home. I did not know why this happened, but I would attempt to find out.

Questions

Before reading further, assume that you are the social worker responsible for engaging Annie for services at the local community healthcare clinic. Homelessness is a pervasive problem that brings with it a constellation of issues and problems unique to this population. Before working with Annie, you must know the current literature on homelessness and treating the homeless.

1. Examine the professional literature regarding homelessness. Describe in detail the problem of homelessness, its prevalence, and break your analysis down by demographic groups (i.e., race, gender, class, etc.).

2. What does the literature state about the various issues and problems faced by homeless individuals? Since you are working in health care, describe the medical and healthcare issues confronting the homeless, particularly young homeless women like Annie.

3. If this were your case, what strategies would you use to engage Annie at the clinic? What does the practice literature say about engaging and working with homeless individuals and families?

When I met Annie, I was the social worker assigned to work with her on behalf of the local community healthcare clinic. I am a white, middle-aged, middle-class, educated mother, with nearly ten years working with the local homeless population and people living with HIV/AIDS. My experience suggested that Annie and I would have to cross many significant cultural differences before we could successfully work together. Yet, my job was to develop a relationship where Annie could trust me as "her social worker."

Often, homeless clients focus on how we can help, more than personal differences. For example, I expected Annie to perceive me as having power in systems where she was powerless. Therefore, she would probably see a relationship with me as being in her best interest. This dynamic was usually enough to "open the door" to a relationship. Moreover, the inherent power imbalance between practitioner and homeless client is constantly part of client relationships. Practitioners must monitor this issue to ensure that homeless clients are not taken advantage of by the system. Practitioners must work with homeless clients in a way that promotes their right to self-determination and informed consent. After all, the homeless have the same rights as other clients under the Code of Ethics (NASW, 2000).

When I approach clients similar to Annie, I ask them to teach me about their life. I do not begin with a series of questions or with a goal of completing my paperwork. Instead, I learn about clients by watching, listening, and linking information slowly as our relationship develops. The homeless, similar to other populations living at the fringes of "normal" society, do not respond well to traditional interviewing, and are averse to responding when the interviewer "interrogates" them. Hence, I use an open-ended interview approach, gleaming relevant personal information from their stories about their life and times. For example, I asked Annie to tell me the story about how she began living in the neighborhood. For the rest of the interview, I asked follow-up questions for more information or clarification.

Social work practitioners must guard against imposing their values, beliefs, and stereotypes onto their clients. Hence, personally and professionally, I needed to recognize my innate desire to rescue people. In the past I demonstrated this by stepping in too quickly to give direction or by interfering with client decision making. I needed to monitor my personal beliefs about what Annie "should do" with her life and recognize that she had the right to decide to take her life in an entirely different direction. Most importantly, I needed to curb my temptation to view Annie as incapable of handling her life. Hence, I needed to avoid the temptation to try controlling her life and decision making. After all, she managed to survive before we met. Annie had skills, resources, and strengths; they simply were not always recognizable to people in the mainstream as such. It is too easy to feel sorry for the homeless, and treating them in a paternalistic manner as if they were children.

Questions

The author just identified her tendencies when working with homeless clients. Since each of us lives in the social world outside our professional practice roles, we come to the job with many preformed attitudes and beliefs about our clients, the nature of their problems, and the role of professional helpers in their lives. Professional education shapes many of our ideas, but not all. Each of us carries into the practice arena attitudes and beliefs that come from our homes, families, and local environments, untouched by the information provided in school. Moreover, as a population, the homeless trigger many differing ideas and political opinions across the United States.

Having negative attitudes and beliefs about particular populations is problematic only when they remain unexplored and unstated. Therefore, for this exercise, answer the following questions as honestly as you can.

1. In a journal format, explore your attitudes and beliefs about homeless individuals. For example, what is your opinion about how people become homeless, why they remain homeless, and what society's role is to help them?

2. This exercise takes courage. Explore the roots of your beliefs, unafraid to write about attitudes and beliefs that run contrary to "social work" values and beliefs. What are the roots of your beliefs about the homeless? Where did these ideas come from, how were they supported, and why do they continue to exist in your life?

3. Engage classmates in a dialogue about the homeless, paying particular attention to the ideas and beliefs that underlie the comments and personal positions of your colleagues.

4. What did you learn about yourself and others? Did this exercise lead to a felt need for corrective action on your part? Explain and defend you answer to this inquiry.

Engaging Annie

Every morning, the clinic's two social workers (I'm one of them) take a daily neighborhood stroll called "rounds." Walking rounds everyday serves several important purposes. First, we locate clients needing to see our volunteer physician that day. We want clients to show for "appointments," since our volunteer time was valuable and limited. We remind clients about their appointments, and offer to transport them to the clinic if required. This usually increases the likelihood that they will show for their appointment.

Second, morning rounds also allow us to survey and greet the homeless community each day. In our city, the homeless community is relatively stable. While most do not perceive this, most homeless residents live in the same neighborhood for years, if not their entire lives. Occasionally, residents move to other communities, but most return; stopping by the clinic to say hello. Morning rounds also give us the opportunity to introduce clinic services to new arrivals and begin informally assessing new people as we meet them.

Third, we get to visit people living in the less visible areas of the homeless community (i.e., empty and dark buildings, under highway bridges, etc.). When approaching these areas, we loudly identify ourselves to ensure safety. However, in my ten years at the clinic, no staff member was attacked or assaulted while walking rounds. We respectfully approach the "camps" to see if anyone was sick or needed help. Occasionally, physicians accompany us to visit reluctant clients needing medical attention. We give the same respect to the "homes" of the residents as we would if we were canvassing homes in a middle class neighborhood. Even homeless people deserve privacy, respect, and dignity.

Like many community members, in the days following our initial greeting, Annie was suspicious of my intentions. She protected herself by watching me interact with others in her community, to make sure that I was honest and trusting. I heard from others that she had been asking around about me, trying to find out if I could be trusted. Trust and consistency are the most important factors when trying to engage members of a homeless community around healthcare services. Many homeless clients expect people to take advantage of them, abuse them, or mislead them with false intentions and empty promises. They are accustomed to people ignoring them, passing them on the streets as if they did not exist. Given their life experiences and frequent interactions with harsh and punitive "helping" systems, I cannot say that I blame them.

I had an additional barrier to overcome with Annie in specific, and the local homeless community in general. Although I had worked at the clinic for a number of years, I did not live in the area, nor had I ever been a homeless person. I was an outsider. To build my reputation, I worked hard over the years at being open, honest, friendly, and accepting. I could not afford to "let down," since I needed to earn the trust of the community everyday. I established my reputation primarily because I was consistent and others in the community spoke highly of me to newcomers. Reputation spreads quickly through the local homeless "grapevine." I learned the importance of keeping my word, being on time, maintaining professional confidences, having a "short memory" regarding missed appointments and/or failure to follow through on the part of residents, and being willing to give something (a free call on my office phone, a referral for a free haircut, a care-kit, or additional time) to clients when needed. In the end, it is simple. To be trusted, practitioners must give trust and act in trustworthy ways.

Gaining trust also means giving trust (Johnson, 2004). I frequently walked the neighborhood with residents, listened to and believed their stories, and asked questions about their lives. When clients and I were together, they were the most important and interesting person in my life. The homeless, like nearly everyone, respond to people genuinely interested in their lives and stories. As stated earlier, most of these people have spent years being treated as if they did not exist. My job was to make them feel welcomed, interesting, and worthwhile. They want to feel important to somebody. On the streets, under bridges, in soup kitchens, and in the clinic, my job was to be that somebody in their lives. This approach helped expand my relationship with clients and minimized our personal differences. As a community healthcare social worker, I learned quickly that my reputation preceded me across their community.

When engaging Annie, I allowed her to progress in our relationship at her own speed. My experience suggests that engagement with clients at homeless clinics often takes multiple visits to collect and/or complete assessment information. Levy (2000) calls the attempts to engage the homeless, particularly those with chronic mental illness, a form of pretreatment. That is, the process of starting new relationships is the most important part of treatment. Levy (2000) refers to this process as similar to the developmental phase of trust versus mistrust. That is, it is the fundamental building block that helping process rests on.

Over the years, I learned to follow a "three times" rule. In other words, my experience suggested that it usually took up to three meetings before a meaningful conversation took place. In this case, I define "meaningful conversation" as including more that a simple "Hi," or "How's it going?" To maintain my patience and not become overbearing, I informally counted the number of contacts with new clients and adjusted my expectations about engagement accordingly.

Levy (2000) supports the idea that a caring and safe presence is necessary to do homeless outreach. Additionally, offering tangible support and/or goods, such as food or a resource, often enhances relationship building. Consistency is another important factor. Local homeless residents saw me in the community nearly everyday, observing the trust other members of the community had for me, and inviting others to stop by the clinic. These factors played an important role in my relationship with Annie. Annie learned that I would do whatever I promised; that she could expect no empty promises in her relationship with me. Levy (2000) states that homeless programs must break out of the traditional mold of service provision and offer a small, secure, low-demand, drop-in model of service. This level of engagement emphasizes the needs of clients and determines the pace and structure of interventions.

Our Second Meeting

Annie came to the clinic a few days after we first met on the street. She tentatively entered the clinic, remaining close to the door in the waiting area. She smiled and greeted the people she knew waiting for services. I saw Annie look toward the front of the lobby in the direction of my office. When she caught my eye, she smiled and said, "I told you I'd come in." This was our second meeting, a positive step indeed. I considered her greeting an indication of a building trust between us. My invitation tempted Annie to come in and explore the clinic. I returned her greeting and kept my distance. She needed to pursue a relationship with me, not the other way around. Besides, my "three times" rule told me that she was not ready to talk yet. I did not want to crowd her and/or threaten her sense of control over how our relationship would develop, if at all. After our brief greeting, she left.

Our Third Meeting and Engagement

I ran into Annie the next day during rounds. She reminded me that she had come to the clinic a day earlier. I made sure that she knew that I saw her and welcomed her back anytime, letting her know that she did not need to have a problem to stop by. Later that day, Annie entered the clinic again. This time, she stood outside my office door and engaged me in short, lighthearted conversation. By her third visit to the clinic at the end of the week (our fourth meeting), Annie walked into my office and sat down in the chair with the office door open. She agreed that it might be a good idea to open a medical record in case she needed help later on. After a short meeting, we tentatively scheduled an appointment for the next week to complete her record. Our relationship was progressing on schedule.

Social Work and the Homeless

Social workers have been part of public healthcare delivery since the beginning of the profession (Moniz & Gorin, 2003). Public health was one of the first targets of social work reform. Jane Addams and other early social work pioneers helped develop early healthcare policies in the United States (Goldberg, 1999; Moniz & Gorin, 2003). Today, social workers in healthcare settings employ an array of skills, including social support, advocacy, education, case management, counseling, health policy development, and social reform.

Understanding the relationship between personal health and the social environment made dramatic progress during the 1940s and 1950s. After World War II, communities learned that certain illnesses were contagious and controllable. Furthermore, we learned that the social environment affected health. A healthy environment was apt to produce a healthy person. In what became known later as the ecological perspective, social workers and public healthcare providers began viewing the person-in-environment. This approach dramatically changed social work practice in the field of health care (Goldberg, 1999).

The ecological perspective led to interest in social determinants theory. This theory proposes that factors such as unemployment, low wages, unaffordable housing, lack of health insurance, racial discrimination, domestic violence, abuse of alcohol and other drugs, and serious mental and physical illnesses play an important role in an individual's health (Evans & Stoddard, 1994). The populations most at-risk for environmentally based health problems include single mothers, the elderly, the poor, the disabled, and the homeless. For the homeless, social determinants play an overwhelming role in health and health care.

Effective healthcare delivery is a recognized national problem, especially for the homeless. Homelessness became a major issue in the late 1970s and early 1980s (Wong, 2002). The de-institutionalization policies of the 1960s flooded cities and rural areas with people who had been institutionalized for decades. Communities and families were poorly equipped to handle the vast array of challenges in offering supportive care. Of the newly released patients, some moved into supervised residential living facilities. Those who did not meet the appropriate criteria for housing or who proved too difficult for residential facilities often became homeless or wound up in jails and prisons.

The homeless population often has higher than average social risks that become barriers to receiving health care (Kushel, Vittinghoff, & Haas, 2001). Many of the homeless have one or more addictions, mental illnesses, or developmental disabilities (Levy, 2000). Some have criminal records. Most are disconnected from their families and support systems despite repeated attempts to establish and maintain relationships. Some report serious mental illness among the homeless to be between 20 and 25 percent (Vamvakas & Rowe, 2001).

In addition, the homeless struggle to receive health care because of the organization and delivery of healthcare services (Rosenbaum & Zuvekas, 2000). The homeless experience a significant challenge when responding to traditional healthcare systems. Lack of money, transportation, and insurance makes access to healthcare systems difficult. Research shows that the homeless seek out health services when it is available, affordable, and accessible (Rosenbaum & Zuvekas, 2000). In many communities across the United States, these are the most significant problems facing the homeless. Our clinic tried to solve these problems in our city.

My Practice Environment

In most cities, everyone knows the homeless neighborhood. The same is true in this medium-sized city. The main street in this neighborhood is highly trafficked and brings workers from the suburbs into the city to work. It occupies some 30 to 40 city blocks, and borders some of the richest developments and high-powered offices in this region of the state. While most consider the neighborhood safe to drive through, few pedestrians walk the streets besides homeless residents. Most city residents consider the homeless neighborhood the place to find drugs, crime, and prostitutes. The neighborhood exists, and everyone knows where it is in the city. However, most drive through it, trying to ignore the people in it.

In this older section of the city, the storefronts show their age. Once home to the finest hotels and stores in the area, what is left are boarded windows, huge real-estate signs, and vacant properties. The most thriving organization in the area is the homeless mission, identified by an oversized cross, secured on the front of the building. Other organizations in the area include a mission store, cheap hotel, and a chapel with a coffee house. A soup kitchen and social gathering place occupies the busiest street corner in the neighborhood. This organization offers the homeless and poor free haircuts, hot meals, and a food pantry.

Our health clinic operates out of a formerly vacant building in the neighborhood. A local hospital manages the clinic, funded through the Stewart B. McKinney Homeless Assistance Act of 1987. The Health Care for the Homeless Program is considered "an indispensable, front-line component of our country's struggle with homelessness" (National Health Care for the Homeless Council [NHCHC], 2003, p. 3). In 1989, our health clinic opened to meet the healthcare needs of the homeless population. The clinic is open everyday from 9:00 a.m. to 5:00 p.m. and is located within a few blocks of the two major missions. It has a large waiting area with comfortable chairs and magazines. The receptionist, nurse, and two social workers comprise the staff. Each has worked at the clinic for more than five years. Consistent personnel are important for trust building in the homeless community, where survival often depends on trust.

In addition, the clinic recruits volunteer physicians from the community who pledge a minimum of 10 hours per month. The physicians represent many subspecialties and many have volunteered for years. The nurse, one volunteer physician, and one social worker speak Spanish. This improves our ability to help the growing Latino population, comprised mainly of migrant workers and their families who use the missions and single room occupancy rentals during nonharvest months. Both social workers, including myself, perform HIV testing and counseling, as well as community education about sexually transmitted diseases.

Our healthcare clinic is a positive intervention at all levels. At a macro level, it meets the emotional needs of the community. By offering a healthcare service that is accessible, humane, and affordable, the community meets the goal of caring for homeless citizens. At the mezzo level, we save the downtown hospitals from having to use the most expensive and least personal way to dispense health care: emergency rooms (Kushel, Perry, Bangsberg, Clark, & Moss, 2002). At the micro level, individuals receive personal care at the clinic. They are more likely to come to the clinic with health and social needs, follow through with treatment recommendations, and receive routine health treatment and prevention.

The homeless require special consideration from social service providers. They do not have transportation, money, or a bed of their own. Missions often insist that residents leave as early as 7:00 a.m. They cannot return until after 4:00 p.m. Therefore, medical orders to "go home and sleep," eat a special diet, and/or to keep medication refrigerated are impossible. The homeless are most interested in meeting their immediate needs such as food, shelter, and safety (Kushel, Vittinghoff, & Haas, 2001). Many may actually avoid health care (NHCHC, 2003). The health clinic meets the needs of the homeless because it is in the neighborhood, offers holistic health care, and develops services to meet the needs of people who are homeless. It is comfortable, nonjudgmental, and familiar. The staff specializes in the healthcare and social needs of the homeless population.

For social workers, healthcare delivery to the homeless is challenging for several reasons. First, the need is enormous and success stories are few. The number of new clients continues to increase, and there is rarely a sense that clients actually move on to a better life. Second, it is frustrating to recognize that our services are better than services at "for pay" health clinics. Health care at these clinics is less convenient, less personal, slower, and less thorough.

As a social worker in a homeless clinic, I learned early that I needed to adjust to constant change and little control over my daily assignments. Practitioners must embrace diversity of all kinds and accept people where and as they are. They must recognize different definitions of success, respect client goals, and resist setting goals for others that reflect practitioner values. These practitioners must learn to celebrate and congratulate success as often as possible. Most people, with or without a home, do the best they can at all times. The same is true for the homeless.

Annie's History

As she promised, Annie came to the healthcare clinic the following week for a meeting. She appeared a little more subdued, and I wondered if she was nervous or tired. I would be tired, too, if I slept in a crowded mission or on the street. I left my office door barely open so Annie would not feel "closed in" or "captured," while still having privacy. I routinely kept the door to my office slightly open when I met with clients because many clients in the clinic experienced paranoid thoughts. If both the client and I felt safe, I would close the door. Homeless clients often experience paranoia because of mental illness, substance abuse, lack of experience in a closed office, fear of community gossip, or because of bad experiences with social work professionals. Relationships will not work if practitioners do not acknowledge this issue and act accordingly.

When I met with Annie, I showed her everything in the file, offered her the papers to hold and look at, and told her why we needed each form and what it required for completion. The more Annie knew about the official and mysterious paperwork in her file, the more comfortable and trusting she would feel. I talked with Annie about confidentiality. I also talked about a "release of information," explaining that unless she signed the form, I could not send her information to any other agency. I also showed Annie our "consent to services" form and told her that she had to sign this form whenever she needed a medical procedure. For our first meeting, I told her that the intake form was most important.

The intake process included a two-page assessment that contained introductory information about clients and documented their homeless status. I completed the assessment through general conversation, getting her to tell me stories about her life. As stated earlier, I did not use a typical question-and-answer format. I usually completed the form over several visits, and Annie was no different. We got about halfway through the form when she decided it was time for her to leave. I also liked to sit so that clients could see what I was writing on their form. Clients often feel less suspicious of the intake process if they can actually see the form.

Below is a summary of Annie's personal information, along with her goals and objectives. We completed her personal history over the course of four visits at the clinic. Each time we met, Annie offered a little more information about herself. I always kept in mind the need to make Annie comfortable, and to allow her to dictate the length of our meetings, where we met, and what information we discussed. Homeless clients have the same right to self-determination and informed consent as clients with homes. They also have the right to be comfortable and feel in control of the information they provide to practitioners.

Presenting Problem(s)

Annie stated that she was healthy and denied having any medical problems. She said that she had rarely visited a doctor, because she was a "healthy girl." However,

Annie did worry about HIV. Since she frequently had unprotected sex with various men in the neighborhood, she wondered if she could "get it." Annie did not use condoms, and wondered if she could get some from me.

Annie also said that she was lonely and alone. Her only substantial social interaction occurred during courtship and sex with the men in the neighborhood. She missed her family and home, and had not made any close friends in the neighborhood. Annie also said that she did not feel safe. Some of the residents in the homeless community frightened her, but she didn't worry as much as some women, because she could "take care" of herself. Annie said—and I had heard—that she was a good "fighter."

Annie's Personal History

Ms. Annie B. was a 19-year-old African American female, currently residing at the Main Cross mission. During our session, Annie maintained good eye contact and followed our conversation well. She was dressed appropriately, was relatively clean, and appeared well nourished. Annie's conversation style was simple and concrete, perhaps indicating a developmental disability. Annie was homeless and eligible for services at the health clinic. She also confirmed that she ate her meals at the soup kitchen and the mission so she had enough food.

Annie was not from the city. She was born and raised in a poor rural community about two hours north of the city. Annie said that the mobile home she lived in with her sister, sister's boyfriend, and mother became "too crowded," so she had to leave. About one month earlier, Annie's sister gave her $50 and a ride to the city, leaving her homeless. Annie found herself alone in a strange city, with no friends or money. She made two collect calls home. However, the last time she called, her sister refused to accept her call. That's when Annie knew that she was really on her own. Annie claimed that she loved her family, and that she had many good memories about childhood. She was not angry with them, but hurt. In weaker moments, Annie expressed her sadness and hurt feelings about being the one that they "put out." According to Annie, they sent her away because the home was crowded and they could not afford to have her living with them. Most of the time, Annie did not seem too upset by this, but she did frequently say that she was lonely and sometimes missed her family.

Annie never knew her father. According to her mother, he was a "bad man" that left immediately after her mother told him that she was pregnant with his baby. Her mother was poor. The family's main source of income over the years was public assistance and money her mother occasionally made prostituting. When Annie was young, her mother would occasionally have her "johns" over to their house during all hours of the day and night. When she was not prostituting herself, her mother had many male friends, but never remarried. Annie said that both her mother and her were "popular" with the "fellows." She seemed to take pride in that fact. She had one sister, who cared for her when her mother could not. Annie was vague and sketchy about her relationships in her family-of-origin. She said that she loved her mother and sister, but that they simply could not care for her any longer.

Annie also liked drinking alcohol with her new "friends." She denied using other drugs and said that she did not have a drinking problem. She said that her drinking sometimes "kind of gets me in trouble," but did not elaborate on this statement. Annie also denied having a substance abuse treatment history. She said that she liked to drink because she made friends easier. She also stated that she needed friends because she felt lonely. Annie reported drinking whenever she could, sometimes everyday, but it was "no big deal."

When she was in school, Annie said that she went to "special class," but did not know why, or what that meant. She could read and write despite not graduating from high school, but was definitely "slow." She was unsure about which grade she completed before dropping out.

Annie was familiar with the term "developmental disability" but was unsure if she "had it." Annie could read slowly and verbalize well, albeit simply and in concrete words and phrases. She was friendly and outgoing with a brilliant smile. There was a simple and naïve quality about her, perhaps making her a target in the homeless community. Annie stated that she was usually optimistic, happy, and always tried to see the positive in others and in situations, regardless of the obstacles.

Annie also said that the men in the neighborhood thought she was attractive. She reveled in their attention, and frequently had sex with these men, sometimes several different men in one day. She said that she liked sex, but mostly liked being popular with the men. She reported that a neighbor "had sex" with her when she was 12 years old, but it was "no big deal." She was also aware that she had gained a reputation for her ability to protect herself, and admitted to being an excellent fighter when she "had to." Annie said that nobody dared try to rape her in the neighborhood, because she would "kick their ass." However, Annie did say that two men had raped her when she was younger. They stopped her on the way home from school and raped her in an abandoned house. That is when she learned to fight.

Her main reason for coming to the health clinic was to get free condoms and learn about HIV. As stated earlier, Annie worried about getting HIV. She knew someone that died of AIDS and knew that "gay people" got it through unprotected sex. She wondered aloud if she might get it, too, despite not being gay. Annie reported no income, but occasionally accepted money from her male friends, and sometimes strangers, for sex. When she needed money, she would offer sexual favors in return for payment, but she did not call herself a prostitute, and I did not ask. Labels are not important, and might only have driven her away. Annie also said that she had trouble finding feminine hygiene products for her menstruation and needed a regular place to "wash."

When I complimented her for coming to the clinic as she promised, Annie said that she always kept her promises, that she was a woman of her word. When we discussed setting personal goals, Annie said that she intended to follow through with her plans. Despite her intentions, my experience suggested that the barriers built-in to a homeless life made following through on good intentions difficult, if not impossible. Realizing and understanding this truth made my work simultaneously interesting and frustrating. She might want to achieve her goals, but life on the streets had an interesting way of getting in the way.

I had heard on the streets that Annie was not always bright and optimistic. Other residents said that sometimes she had "spells." They said she became moody, angry, and acted strangely. I asked Annie about this, and she said that she had them, but they were "no big deal." She said that she gets sad and does not want to be bothered. She did not know why she had them, but she knew that she did, and always had since she was a little girl. Given that our relationship was new, I decided against pushing this conversation any further.

Questions

Now that the author has presented information about Annie's life, and before reading on, perform the following exercises based on your education, experience, the professional literature, and best practice evidence. To increase the learning potential of this exercise, you may want to do this in a small group with other students in your course.

1. Based on the information in this case, construct a three-generation genogram and eco-map that represents Annie's personal, familial, and environmental circumstances. What further information do you need to complete this exercise? What patterns do these two important graphical assessment tools demonstrate?

2. Write a complete list of Annie's issues and strengths.

3. Write a two- to three-page narrative assessment that encompasses Annie's multi-systemic issues and strengths. Review Chapter 1 if needed. This narrative should provide a comprehensive and multi-systemic explanation of her life as she prepares to work with the author.

4. Try to identify the theoretical model or approach that you use to guide your assessment. According to the literature, what other theoretical options are available and how would these change the nature of your assessment?

5. The author did not provide a clinical diagnosis. However, as a student you should take every opportunity to practice this process. Therefore, develop multi-axial DSM-IV-TR diagnoses based on the information provided above and in your assessment narrative. Be sure to look for evidence of multiple diagnoses on Axis I. Provide the list of client symptoms that you used to justify your diagnostic decisions. What, if any, information was missing that would make this an easier task?

6. Explore the practice literature to find what approaches are best suited for working with clients with Annie's issues and strengths. What special issues

must you consider for treatment that encompasses the various issues in Annie's life?

7. Develop a treatment plan with goals and objectives that is based on Annie's unique circumstances, your narrative assessment, diagnoses, and the practice literature. Compare your treatment recommendations to other's in your class and seek to understand any differences that arise.

Treatment Planning: Annie's Goals and Objectives

Annie and I developed her personal goals and objectives together during our meetings. We used her goals to guide our work. I intended to help Annie find ways to solve her problems and improve her life. I had clients state their goals in the first-person in an effort to encourage personal ownership and increase their motivation.

Goal 1: *I am concerned about sexually transmitted infections, such as HIV.*

Objectives:
1. Reduce my risk of becoming infected with HIV through reducing harmful behaviors.
2. Attend HIV counseling and education and consider HIV testing.
3. Identify my risks for HIV and think of ideas for me to reduce my risk of infection.
4. Talk to the clinic nurse about having a physical.

Goal 2: *I am worried about violence, crime, and substance abuse because I am a young woman living in the missions and drinking with strangers.*

Objectives:
1. Work with clinic to find housing.
2. Work with clinic to receive subsidized housing allowance.
3. Work with clinic to get on a housing waiting list for subsidized housing.

Goal 3: *I am often lonely and need someone to talk to that I can trust.*

Objectives:
1. Drop by the clinic to find a safe place to talk.
2. Work with clinic social worker to solve day-to-day problems.
3. Work with clinic social worker to find a women's group to find friends.

Notice that I did not include objectives designed to examine her drinking. I suspected that she might be underreporting her alcohol use, mainly because of the people she associated with in the local community. I was familiar with her friends' drinking habits and suspected that she drank much more than she stated. However, Annie was not interested in exploring this issue. To insist on this as a problem would have risked driving her away from her newly forming relationships at the clinic. Hence, I believe that treatment goals and objectives must be client driven, and match their personal desires and wishes, not mine. However, this did not mean that I would ignore the issue; I simply was unprepared to demand that she deal with it at this time.

Questions

1. **Compare the treatment plan you established with the author's treatment plan. What differences and similarities exist between the plans? How do you account for the differences? Use the professional literature and practice evidence to analyze both plans, and the differences between them.**

2. **Develop a revised treatment plan from information provided by the author, your original plan, and the practice literature. What does the evidenced-based practice literature say are the most effective ways to treat clients with Annie's problems and strengths? Using the rationale from the literature and your experience, develop a position on this issue.**

Annie's Treatment

I approached Annie the same way that I approached all new clients. I assumed that she was trying her best to cope with being homeless and deal with her difficult childhood, not to mention having been "turned out" by her family because she was a burden. At 19 years old, her family forced Annie into homelessness to live alone in a new environment where it was easier to find alcohol, other drugs, and sex than food. She lived in an environment where she could be assaulted, beaten, or raped daily or while sleeping. Homeless clients also face stigma everyday of their lives, from nearly everyone they meet. The last thing Annie needed was for me to see her as incapable, morally bankrupt, or bad. She got that from others. I needed to be different, see her differently, and base my approach on her strengths and not her deficits. Perhaps more than "help," Annie needed me to recognize her as a human being with feelings, desires, and ideas. She needed to be a real person, and not a helpless or lazy statistic that most in "normal" society would rather ignore.

As stated above, since I suspected that Annie underreported her drinking and sex life, and that these issues were an important part of her long-term health and well-being, I approached her carefully. Therefore, I decided to take a harm reduction approach, hoping to help Annie make incremental changes in her drinking and frequency of unprotected sex, in an effort to reduce the potential for harm these behaviors might cause. At the same time, I worked with Annie toward finding new living arrangements that would ultimately make her life safer and more secure. This is the essence of a harm reduction model (Marlatt, 1998).

Harm reduction models offer strategies for managing high-risk behaviors such as substance abuse and HIV transmission, while working toward long-term change. The goal of harm reduction is to meet people "where they are at" and help them reduce the possibility of harm associated with their behavior. Harm reduction applies several important principles, including:

1. Drug use is part of our world and it is necessary to reduce harmful effects, rather than condemn it, ignore it, or demand that it cease.
2. Drug users have a voice in their treatment.
3. Drug use is complex and multifaceted, existing on a continuum of behaviors, from abstinence to abuse.
4. Work toward improved quality of life and well-being by reducing the potential for harm. It is possible for clients to make changes and reduce harm, even while using drugs, drinking, or engaging in other harmful behaviors.
5. Requires practitioners to be nonjudgmental and noncoercive when providing services and resources to clients.
6. Recognizes the realities of poverty, class, racism, social isolation, past trauma, sex-based discrimination, and other social inequalities that affect vulnerability and the capacity to deal with one's problems.
7. Does not minimize or ignore the real and tragic harms and dangers associated with substance abuse (Harm Reduction Coalition, 1996).

Levy (2000) recognizes that the homeless are at an increased risk of substance and physical abuse because of their isolation from community resources, poverty, and disenfranchisement from society. Annie was indeed isolated from her community and family. I tried to link her with basic needs such as housing, food, education, social support, and medical services. This approach offered Annie help in the context of an accepting environment that supported her work toward solving her problems, her right to practice self-determination, and the initiative to reach her goals.

In other words, since it was unlikely that Annie would soon find a house and job or stop drinking and having sex, given her circumstances, my job was to minimize the potential for harm that were inherent in her existing environment. I provided free condoms and HIV education in an effort to help Annie realize that she could protect herself against sexually transmitted diseases. We offered her opportunities to have an HIV test, mental health services, provided education about alcohol abuse, and worked to find her appropriate housing in an effort to reduce the potential for risk in her life. I provided the services she wanted while continually working to engage her so that if she ever decided to deal with her other problems, she would have a safe place and a trusted person to talk with about these issues.

Questions

1. Take a moment to review the author's treatment approach. Based on the author's description, the professional literature, and the latest practice evidence, state and defend your opinion about her approach.

2. Examine the literature for information about harm reduction as a treatment approach. Based on the literature, your experience, and your personal beliefs about helping, state and defend your position on harm reduction models in practice.

3. Based on the work you completed earlier, what additional approach or approaches would you recommend? Use the literature and latest practice evidence to justify your recommendations.

Annie's Story

I worked with Annie for nearly three years, from the day of our first meeting on the street until the day I left for new employment. Annie came to the clinic frequently, usually once a week. She often came to talk with me about relationship problems with boyfriends or her family. I suspected that Annie might also have a diagnosable mental disorder, substance abuse problem, and/or health problems, but she protected herself from considering these issues. Moreover, she resisted any efforts to refer her for mental health services (see below).

As I knew Annie better, I began seeing her "spells." One day she would present as a bright and cheery person, the next would be different. I noticed that she would frequently change moods and seem to lose her ability to express or show her emotions. She would become sullen, hostile, and show blunted affect. During these periods, Annie became quiet and less interactive. She lost interest in her surroundings and self-care, would stay away from the clinic, and seemingly drop from sight around the neighborhood. I worried about her during these periods.

At first, I suspected depression. However, her mood changes happened quickly and usually lasted a month or so; suggesting that she was probably not depressed. I also wondered about the possibility of a Dissociative Disorder, given her circumstances, environment, and upbringing. However, this is difficult to diagnose, because other disorders often appear similar to a dissociative disorder. These include schizophrenia, bipolar disorder, anxiety disorders, and personality disorders (American Psychiatric Association, 2000). Dissociative disorder is a complicated diagnosis that requires a medical consult. As a social worker, I can make diagnostic impressions and recommendations. In my state, only medical doctors can make final diagnoses.

Question

Now that you have a more complete description of Annie's "spells," refer to the DSM-IV-TR (APA, 2000) and attempt to diagnose her spells. Be sure to list the qualifying criteria used to make your diagnosis.

I scheduled Annie to meet with a physician at the clinic. After the meeting, our physician decided that Annie needed a psychiatric consultation, and referred her to the mental health clinic in the community. Our physician wanted to make sure that a trained psychiatrist assessed, diagnosed, and treated her. He thought that her problem was too serious for an internist to handle.

When the day arrived for her appointment, I could not find her. She was either hiding or had disappeared. I had the same problem three times. When I asked about her disappearance right before mental health appointments, Annie claimed that her "spells" were "no big deal" and they had happened most of her life and did not bother her at all. Obviously, Annie hid as a way to miss her appointments with Community Mental Health. My concern was that her "spells" made Annie more vulnerable on the streets and later made it difficult for her to function in subsidized housing. This issue remained a mystery and frustration for me. Annie was not motivated to fix her "spells."

With Annie's permission, I obtained her education records. Because the school had diagnosed her with a developmental disability, we used her records to help Annie qualify for disability payments and medical coverage. With her new income, Annie was able to afford her own apartment, a vast improvement in her living condition.

Termination

I decided to leave the clinic for different employment. This was difficult for many clients, but especially for Annie. I tried to sit down with her and explain why I was leaving. I wanted to link her with the other social worker for the future. However, I could not find her anywhere. I tried to find her for three weeks, but Annie did not come to the clinic and she did not show up during rounds. Everyone at the clinic wondered if Annie disappeared as her way of avoiding termination, since everyone in the neighborhood knew that I was leaving. The residents threw me a "good-bye" party. Most likely, Annie did not want to terminate. Neither did I, really.

Annie did not change her goals in the three years I knew her, but she did accomplish some of them. Most importantly, Annie maintained a safe and trusting relationship with me for three years. The clinic's nurse treated various infections and Annie solved several daily life issues with me in a safe environment.

Annie continued to have relationships with men and women that placed her in vulnerable situations. Often they would come into the neighborhood to sell drugs, particularly during the first week of the month when disability checks arrived. At times, Annie would fight. However, most of the time, she "hung out" and enjoyed the attention and gifts the relationships brought her. She continued to drink regularly, but also continued to deny that it was a problem for her. Annie stated that she understood the transmission of HIV and that she insisted on condoms during intercourse.

We never treated Annie for her "spells." I regretted being unable to get her to accept medical help for this condition. I always wondered if medication would have helped. I hope that someone else connected her with the appropriate professional helpers.

I liked Annie. When not in a spell, she was optimistic and positive about life. She tried hard to do her best and felt bad and apologetic when she thought she disappointed me or other staff at the clinic. She looked for approval and support from others. Yet, her ability to accept adult responsibility always seemed just beyond her grasp.

I occasionally see Annie walking in the homeless neighborhood. I wonder if she continues to experience periods of stability followed by periods of instability. She did maintain herself in independent living, mainly because her landlord liked her when she was not drinking or having a "spell." I hope Annie connected with another social worker at the clinic so she had someone she could talk with and trust.

Annie always spoke affectionately of her family "back home," but there was never any evidence of the family meeting with her or giving her any attention. Her "new family" was a group of people who recognized her strengths and cheered her on toward her goal of a safe and happy life. I am sure that Annie would identify the staff at the clinic as part of her new family.

Questions

The author presented an interesting case that involved many issues commonly found in medical social work practice with homeless clients. Taking a broad view of this case, reevaluate the author's work and your participation through the questions asked throughout the case.

1. **Overall, what is your professional opinion of the work performed in this case? As always, refer to the professional literature, practice evidence, your experience, and the experience of student-colleagues when developing your opinion.**

2. **Based on this review, what additional or alternative approaches could she have used with this case? That is, if you were the practitioner, how would you have approached this case? Please explain and justify your approach.**

3. **What did this case demonstrate that you could use in other practice settings? List the most important things you learned and how you could apply these lessons in your practice career.**

Bibliography

American Psychiatric Association (2000). *Diagnostic and statistical manual of mental disorders* (4th ed., TR). Washington DC: Author.

Evans, R. G., & Stoddard, G. L. (1994). Producing health, consuming health care. In P. R. Lee and D. L. Estes, (eds.), *The Nation's Health* (4th ed., pp. 14–33). Boston: Jones and Bartlett.

Goldberg, J. (1999). A short-term approach to intervention with homeless mothers: A role for clinicians in homeless shelters. *Families in Society, 80*(2), 161–168.

Harm Reduction Coalition [HRC]. (1996). *Mission and principles of harm reduction* [Brochure]. Oakland, CA: Author.

Johnson, J. L. (2004). *Fundamentals of substance abuse practice.* Pacific Grove, CA: Brooks/Cole.

Kushel, M., Perry, S., Bangsberg, D., Clark, R., & Moss, A. (2002). Emergency department use among the homeless and marginally housed: Results from a community-based study. *American Journal of Public Health, 92*(5), 778–784.

Kushel, M., Vittinghoff, E., & Haas, J. (2001). Factors associated with the health care utilization of homeless persons. *The Journal of the American Medical Association, 285*(2), 200–206.

Levy, J. (2000). Homeless outreach: On the road to pretreatment alternatives. *Families in Society, 81*(4), 360–368.

Marlatt, G. A. (Ed.). (1998). *Harm reduction: Pragmatic strategies for managing high-risk behaviors.* New York: The Guilford Press.

Moniz, C., & Gorin, S. (2003). *Health and health care policy: A social work perspective.* Boston: Allyn and Bacon.

National Association of Social Workers. (2000). *The Code of Ethics for the National Association of Social Workers.* Washington, DC: Author.

National Health Care for the Homeless Council [NHCHC]. Because health care is a right, not a privilege. Retrieved July 14, 2003 from http://www.nhchc.org/Publications/basics-of-home lessness.htm.

Rosenbaum, S., & Zuvekas, A. (2000). Healthcare use by homeless persons: Implications for public policy. *Health Services Research, 34*(6), 1303–1305.

Vamvakas, A., & Rowe, M. (2001). Mental health training in emergency homeless shelters. *Community Mental Health Journal, 37*(3), 287–295.

Wong, Y. I. (2002). Tracking change in psychological distress among homeless adults: An examination of the effect of housing status. *Health & Social Work, 27*(4), 262–273.

5

Mrs. Smith and Her Family

Doreen R. McGrath

Introduction

The following case study provides an excellent example of the various roles and responsibilities of a medical social worker working primarily in a hospital setting. It is a challenging and fast-paced field of practice, demanding a variety of skills needed to negotiate multiple environments to serve our clients. I have worked at a large hospital in a medium-sized city for nearly eight years. While the work can be frustrating, it is always exciting and varied. Given the range of cases and issues that I see everyday, I find hospital social work satisfying. Yet, as you will see in the case study below, sometimes these systems and people interact to make my work difficult and challenging.

As stated above, the following case examines the various challenges a hospital social worker faces during a typical workday. It also demonstrates how quickly a hospital social worker's plan might change, along with the different approaches used to interact with the various people involved in every case. Hospital social workers must know how to respond to crises, during a confrontation, and/or with intense grief reactions. Practitioners must work with people who are overprotective, poor family historians, manipulative, psychotic, demanding, or timid. The variety makes work interesting. Moreover, practitioners must remain self-aware to avoid becoming someone their clients cannot trust. If this occurs, people do not receive the help they need.

Mrs. Smith

Mrs. Smith was an eighty-year-old African American woman, sent to our hospital one evening by the staff at her nursing home. She experienced shortness of breath and almost immediately lost consciousness. The doctors in the emergency room surmised that she had a stroke. Mrs. Smith was in grave danger because of ill health complicated by her age and preexisting medical conditions.

Obviously, Mrs. Smith was unable to provide her own medical history and her family was not at the hospital at the time of her admission. The medical team learned from her nursing home record that Mrs. Smith had recently suffered a cerebral vascular accident (stroke). To recover, she lived in a nursing home where she received rehabilitation and the twenty-four-hour health care needed to meet her medical needs. Her record also revealed that she was diagnosed with dementia prior to her stroke. As it turned out, Mrs. Smith was unable to meet her basic needs even before having the stroke three months earlier. Oddly, the nursing home did not list any family contacts in her record.

Within a few moments of her admission to our facility, Mrs. Smith's medical condition worsened. Her status became life-threatening and doctors placed her on a ventilator and immediately transferred her to the intensive care unit for close medical monitoring. Mrs. Smith was in serious medical distress.

Despite Mrs. Smith's inability to consent for treatment and in the absence of family, hospital personnel may act on a client's behalf during an emergency without formal consent. According to Showalter (1999), "an emergency eliminates the need to obtain consent because the law values the preserving of life and prevention of permanent impairment to health" (p. 352).

Hospital Social Work

Before returning to Mrs. Smith's case, I would like to share a brief overview of hospital social work. Social work practice in a hospital setting offers unique and satisfying challenges in a hectic and fast-paced environment. It provides social workers the chance to interact simultaneously with multiple systems using various methods of treatment. Perhaps the biggest challenge involves balancing social work responsibilities with the multi-systemic hospital environment, including laws and policies, legal issues, and the issues presented by patients and their families. This requires quick thinking, adaptability, and willingness to compromise.

From a multi-systemic framework (see Chapter 1), hospital social workers interface with macro-level regulations from the federal government and the legal system, mezzo-level criteria as implemented by hospital policy and local healthcare organizations and institutions, and micro-level interactions with patients and families. To be effective in this environment, practice demands brief intervention combined with short-term case management, an understanding of relevant laws and policies, and familiarity with funding and managed care providers. I only see most patients and/or family members once or twice before they discharge. Because my practice time line is brief, I must rapidly engage people to complete an assessment and develop a discharge plan. During their stay, a hospital social worker's primary function is to provide patients and families with emotional support while helping them move through the health system, from admission through discharge.

Hospitalization often represents a major life-changing event for patients and their families. Many patients and families that I meet are in dire circumstances. A large number are facing their death or the death of a loved one. Patients might receive a terminal cancer diagnosis or they might have been in an accident and suffered paralysis. A psychiatric disorder might have prompted a suicide attempt. An elderly patient's worsening medical condition might lead to nursing home placement or withdrawal from life support. Additionally, patients and their families vary greatly in their ways of coping with major life stressors. We help people adjust to their new life and the issues demanded by their new circumstances.

Hospital social workers see a variety of cases, often on the same day. In my seven years of service, I have never lost interest working with clients in the hospital setting because of the daily variety and professional challenges.

Practitioner's Role

Hospital social workers contribute to patient care as a member of a team of professionals. My goal as a social worker is to complete a psychosocial assessment, deal with any existing emotional needs during treatment, as well as design and implement a safe and accurate discharge plan when patients are medically stable. The healthcare team at our hospital consists of various professionals including physicians, nurses, physical therapists, occupational therapists, and speech therapists. These and other professionals attend to the patient's medical and emotional needs in an environment of limited resources. These days, financial considerations play an important role in most healthcare decisions. Medicare, Medicaid, private insurers, and HMOs (health maintenance organizations) greatly influence the utilization of services for their enrollees.

Utilization Review

Because of the emphasis on cost containment, social workers work closely with the utilization review team to ensure a safe and timely discharge within the guidelines of the patient's funding source. The role and function of utilization review is to make recommendations about the need and appropriateness of continued hospitalization for individual patients. The impact of the committee's recommendation is primarily financial: when the committee determines that a patient's medical condition no longer warrants hospitalization, a third-party payer frequently discontinues payment for inpatient care (Showalter, 1999). This applies significant pressure on healthcare teams to meet a patient's medical, emotional, and discharge needs in a timely manner and, hopefully, under budget. Hence, hospitals work diligently to monitor length of stay and to discharge patients when acute care services are no longer necessary.

Utilization review is one of many attempts to decrease healthcare costs. According to Showalter (1999), "In recent years third-party payers and healthcare providers have developed various kinds of managed care organizations (MCOs) as a means of controlling the costs of care and in response to the competitive environment" (p. 288). Because insurers can deny payment, hospital personnel closely monitor patient length of stay in the hospital. The hospital discharges patients once their medical condition requires a less costly environment. Whereas in previous eras, patients were often given extra time in the hospital to ensure recovery. Today, that is not the case. Patients are discharged immediately after becoming stable enough to leave.

Questions

Similar to all areas of practice, managed care and organized cost containment measures have affected the way hospitals provide services. As the author stated, as soon as patients are medically stable and able to move, they are discharged home or to lower-cost, less intensive placements in the community. Many practitioners in social work and health care believe that managed care has weakened the system and placed patients and families at risk. Others believe that managed care makes efficient use of limited resources to provide care for the greatest number of people possible. Nonetheless, this remains a hot topic across the healthcare delivery system.

1. Examine the professional literature regarding managed care and its affects on healthcare delivery, including social work services. During this investigation, be sure to explore any outcome studies that compare treatments in and out of managed care environments. Write a critical essay, demonstrating the findings from the literature that ends with you taking a definitive position about the value of managed care in healthcare and social service delivery systems.

2. Examine the code of professional ethics (NASW, 2000) to determine how social workers should approach issues that arise because of managed care. Present all sides of your arguments and attempt to develop a process for using the code of ethics to evaluate treatment and discharge decisions.

3. Engage with classmates in a dialogue about this topic. Managed care and client funding will be a significant part of professional practice. Listen intently for the different opinions and beliefs about the impact of managed care on the profession.

Helping Patients Navigate Health Care

In addition to the financial emphasis, Aiken (1991) reports, "the relatively impersonal, technology-based modern hospital with its busy atmosphere oriented primarily toward curing illness and prolonging life does not always permit the implementation of humanitarian principles" (p. 221). It is the social worker's job to ensure that patients and their families do not become lost or overwhelmed in this intimidating environment. Working from a systems perspective, hospital social workers attempt to restore a patient's dignity during this stressful and vulnerable time. It is important to remember the personal aspects of hospital social work practice.

Too often, hospital personnel refer to patients as a room number or a diagnosis. Social workers cannot. They are the first line of defense against patient and family alienation and intimidation, representing the humanistic element of the healthcare system. Social workers listen to patient stories, learn about their fears, recognize their part of a complex system, support them through the hospitalization, and ease their transition back home or onto their next level of care.

The health system that I work for has combined social work with nurse utilization managers to coordinate discharge planning. Nurses carry out the utilization review function and discharge patients with complex medical needs. This often includes planning discharge for patients who need feeding tube supplies, wound dressing supplies, or chemo-dialysis, and so on. Nurses do an excellent job of answering medical questions related to a patient's discharge plan. For example, patients need to know how to self-administer a shot of insulin if they have a new diagnosis of diabetes. This is something that social workers cannot do.

In our system, social workers become involved with patients who have psychosocial issues. For example, I commonly work with patients with a new diagnosis of cancer, a suicide attempt, alcoholism, death and dying, and patients with psychiatric illness. In our hospital system, social workers, regardless of their areas of practice, complete assessments, establish interventions, and make referrals. Because of the fast-paced nature of the work and setting, hospital social workers condense these processes. This pace requires that I be fast while not overlooking patients and their family needs because of the speed with which I must do my work.

I find that performing social work in the hospital's fast-paced environment requires a strengths-based approach. This approach focuses on client resources and strengths in their multi-systemic environment to help patients achieve their goals (Johnson, 2004). Our environment does not allow time to focus too long on client problems or deficits. I attempt to empower patients and families to take charge of their situations and make decisions in their lives. Hence, I work to organize family support networks and, when applicable, other healthcare or rehabilitation organizations to give patients the best chance for success after discharge. Empowering patients and families to be self-sufficient is an important component to helping with personal adjustment after a medical issue or crisis. As Turner (1986) explained,

> In the role of the enabler, the social workers carry out the tasks of mobilizing or strengthening motivation to deal with the stress of life transitions and helping to manage the disabling feeling and maintain self-esteem. (p. 630)

The process of helping patients and families recognize and utilize their strengths to help meet their needs is empowering. Commonly, the technology of medicine, the medical jargon, or fear of the unknown involving their illness intimidates patients and their families. This often leads to feelings of isolation and vulnerability at a critical time when patients need comfort and reassurance. My job is to help patients overcome their fears.

For example, imagine you are a patient needing one of your limbs amputated. Medical staff might claim that you need to go to a rehabilitation facility after surgery before you can safely return home, and the only rehabilitation facilities with available openings are across town from where your family lives. After you reluctantly agree to rehabilitation, the hospital transfers you to the new facility with new staff and new expectations. Moreover, you worry about whether you will be well enough to return home before maximizing your insurance benefits. My job is to demystify this process and help ensure that patients are ready and able to face these changes in a way that maximizes their energies for the hard work ahead.

Hospital social workers also help patients transition back into the community. Although it can be a frightening and traumatic experience coming to the hospital, it can be even more frightening to leave. The previous example demonstrates how overwhelming, stressful, and depressing post-surgery options can become. I primarily address the emotional issues that result from the stress and change after hospitalization. My job is to listen, validate, encourage, teach, empower, and apply professional use of "self" to affect lives. It is important for social workers to rely on "self" to be effective in any practice setting.

A Variety of Roles and Specialties

Below I briefly discuss the variety of specialties and roles that social workers perform in hospital settings. This list is not intended as an exhaustive list. Social workers in hospitals play a number of roles and support different medical subspecialties.

An oncology social worker works with people newly diagnosed with cancer, in treatment for cancer, or dying of cancer. Therefore, oncology social workers work with people losing their hair, their strength, and possibly their lives. Grief and loss, death and dying, and patient and family support are just a few of the factors these social workers would address on a daily basis.

A surgical social worker sees people after surgery. He or she helps people adjust to decreased abilities or, perhaps, an amputation. These social workers might see people going through situational depression due to significant lifestyle changes because of their surgery.

An orthopedic social worker works with elderly patients who come into the hospital with broken hips or broken arms, and so on. They often work with patients and families adjusting to the reality that their loved one cannot return home because of limited mobility or an inability to care for themselves. These workers frequently must arrange nursing home placements and deal with the grieving associated with people having to give up their home and loss of independence.

A cardiology social worker sees people who come into the hospital with heart problems or chest pain because of a heart attack or drug use. These social workers also work with depression, a common side effect of a heart attack. They may also work with patients abusing drugs and try to connect them to treatment programs.

A pediatric social worker works with children and their families for a variety of conditions. They may need to involve child protective services if they suspect child abuse or neglect. These social workers also work with reluctant mothers who need reassurance about their ability to care for their newborn baby or mothers experiencing post-partum depression.

A neurological social worker works with patients who suffer from seizures, migraines, or a stroke. These social workers might work with patients who have residual deficits from a stroke or paralysis. Loss of independence and depression are important factors that these social workers face.

An emergency room social worker is on the frontlines dealing with any crisis presented at the hospital. These social workers work with patients who have been in a motor vehicle accident, victims of domestic violence, victims of violence, or the homeless who often present in the emergency room intoxicated.

The Smith Family: Client Engagement

Given her medical condition at the time of admittance, Mrs. Smith was in no condition to speak with me. She was unconscious and barely clinging to life. As the social worker for Mrs. Smith, I needed to meet with responsible family members to collect client and family information and complete an assessment. When I was assigned to Mrs. Smith, she was already on the ventilator and unable to communicate.

As I entered her room, I noticed a frail, elderly man napping in a bedside chair. It was Mr. Smith, my client's husband. According to Mrs. Smith's nurse, his niece had dropped him off earlier and then left. I slowly approached Mr. Smith, introduced myself, and engaged him in a brief conversation. I discovered that while he was oriented to person (he knew who he and his wife were), he was disoriented related to place (where am I?), time (what day is it?), and situation (what is happening, why am I here?). That is, Mr. Smith knew that his wife was in the bed next to him, but did not know why or how she got there. Interestingly, he also did not know where his wife was living prior to her admission. I surmised that Mr. Smith also had dementia and would not be able to assist with my assessment.

Later, Mrs. Smith's niece finally returned to the hospital. When I approached her, she clearly was agitated. She was pacing and loudly demanding answers. I found her difficult to engage or talk to in her highly charged emotional state. She was clearly in crisis and making a scene in the hallway just outside Mrs. Smith's room. To minimize disruptions to other patients, I quickly escorted her to a conference room so that we could have privacy.

In a crisis such as this, "the worker needs to establish quick rapport in order to elicit needed information quickly and to inspire confidence that he can help" (Turner, 1986, p. 317). This was my task with Mrs. Smith's niece. I needed to deescalate her intense emotional state to help her process her feelings so that she could better cope with her stress at that moment. Therefore, I approached her in a calm and direct manner. In time, I established rapport with her and helped redirect her fear so that we could converse about Mrs. Smith's situation. Within a few minutes, her tone of voice softened and her anxiety subsided. Soon, we were conversing calmly and she expressed her concerns appropriately.

Questions

The client presentation described above is common. One family member (the patient) is in significant crisis and others are emotionally distraught and impatient, looking for immediate answers to their questions. Imagine you were the social worker assigned this case and answer the following questions before moving ahead.

1. What is your first hunch regarding this case? Explore the practice literature and discuss this issue with other students to identify any relevant issues that you should consider with the Smith family.

2. What is the next direction of inquiry and assessment? Further, explore the practice literature to locate theories or models that apply to this type of work. Based on what you find, what information would you need to collect to perform a comprehensive and/or multi-systemic assessment? (See Chapter 1).

3. What personal strengths can you locate and name at this early juncture in treatment?

Diversity and Culture

As stated above, Mrs. Smith was an African American woman. I am a Caucasian woman, married, with one child. Therefore, I needed to approach the Smith family in a way that demonstrated my ability to understand and engage them in a culturally competent manner.

Having worked with many African American families regarding death and treatment, I knew that some families overtly express their sadness, grief, and frustration related to grief over sickness and/or death. Moreover, many African American families rely heavily on prayer, church, and extended family for support and guidance. Hence, I needed to inquire about their religious preference and involvement, since the spiritual aspect of a person's life can be central to how they respond to medical management.

While the factors stated above may generally be consistent in the African American community, I could not assume that they represented the Smith family. As you will read below, the Smith family did rely extensively on extended family support, but they declined my offer to involve a minister from their church. Moreover, while Mrs. Smith's niece was highly emotional in the early stages of their crisis, this could have been a normal reaction to a life-or-death crisis for anyone from any racial and cultural background and not an indication of something specific pertaining to African Americans.

Social workers must view families individually, locating each patient and family's unique characteristics. It is offensive to draw conclusions about people based on their ethnic group or stereotype. Hospital employees should be sensitive to individuality as they interface with people struggling with death, something everyone approaches differently despite their ethnic backgrounds.

Questions

As the author stated, social workers and other professional helpers must approach clients in a culturally competent manner (see Chapter 1). She provided two issues from her experience that she considered relevant in this case. Respond to the following questions, given the rich, emerging literature in the profession about cultural competence and human diversity.

1. **Explore the literature to find other culturally and/or racially relevant issues that you would consider if you were working with the Smith family. List these issues.**

2. **Examine what the literature says about the issues presented by the author. Did the literature reflect the author's practice experience? Explain what you found and compare it to the author's analysis of the situation with the Smith family.**

3. **If you were preparing to engage the Smiths, what would your overall approach entail in order to provide culturally competent services to this family?**

Finding a Surrogate Decision Maker

Mrs. Smith's niece was primarily concerned about how the family would appoint Mrs. Smith's medical power of attorney. The family knew of no previously signed documents or plans for this eventuality. Mr. Smith, the niece's actual blood relative, did not know of any previous arrangement either. Her anxiety was specifically related to this important issue in the family.

A medical power of attorney is the legal decision maker, appointed by patients to speak on their behalf when they are unable to speak or become unable to make important personal decisions. Often, families have made these decisions and arrangements prior to entering the hospital. This is especially true in families with elderly members. Unfortunately, Mrs. Smith was unable to declare a power of attorney because of her current incapacitation. She was in no condition to make an informed decision about something this important. Further, the niece explained that Mr. Smith was unable to be Mrs. Smith's decision maker because of his poor memory, impaired thought process, and his own inability to make rational decisions. Moreover, he was unable to appoint someone to fulfill this role on his wife's behalf.

As I explored her concerns further, I learned about significant family problems that played a role in this issue. Mrs. Smith's niece stated that Mr. Smith was
his wife's second husband. After Mrs. Smith went into the nursing facility, the two
extended families of each spouse agreed that each would care for their respective
family member. According to the niece, the extended families did not get along, so
they decided to stay out of each other's business now that both Mr. and Mrs. Smith
were incapacitated. While the two extended families had no contact with each other,
here I was talking to Mr. Smith's blood relative about how to appoint Mrs. Smith's
power of attorney, despite their agreement to allow Mrs. Smith's blood relations to
care for her.

As I learned shortly, Mrs. Smith had one daughter, Tammy, two adult grand-
daughters, and one great grandchild. The niece was actually more concerned about
finding help for Mr. Smith, now that it looked like his wife was terminally ill. She
wanted help getting Mr. Smith into the same nursing home as Mrs. Smith. I provided her with the information she needed to begin that process.

As the emotional crisis subsided, I supplemented my crisis intervention work
with elements of the systems model. As Turner (1986) explained, "this perspective
has a particular relevance for intervention in crisis situations because of its emphasis on assessment that takes into account the variety of aspects of the person-in-sit-
uation" (p. 534). This proved helpful in this case. The niece was forthcoming with
information about Mr. Smith and herself. This provided insight into Mr. Smith's
extended family's level of involvement with Mrs. Smith, and began my process of
learning about Mrs. Smith's family and life circumstances.

In hospital social work, when patients are incompetent, we assist the healthcare team to identify alternative decision makers. "When the patient cannot speak
voluntarily because of incompetence, the law demands that someone in the proper
position of authority speak as surrogate" (Showalter, 1999, p. 335). Therefore, my
initial focus was to establish a surrogate decision maker for Mrs. Smith. Medically,
Mrs. Smith's condition stabilized with the support of a ventilator. Because she was
currently in a life-or-death situation, I, with the support of my supervisor, ruled out
an immediate need for a court-appointed temporary guardian.

Questions

**As someone preparing to work in medical social work, the legalities and ethics
involved with power of attorney rights and legal guardianship are important
issues to grasp. Respond to the following questions before reading further in
this case.**

**1. Explore the literature to find information on the legal requirements for
guardianship and power of attorney in your state or country. Specifically, what
are the criteria to determine when a surrogate decision maker is needed, and
what steps must you take to arrange this with an incapacitated or legally
incompetent patient's family?**

2. Given the particulars of this case at this point, what is your opinion about the author's approach and decisions in this case? What hunches do you currently have about the relations between the extended families and the role this might play in the future of this case?

3. Referring to an earlier discussion about cultural competence, what does the literature say about appointing surrogate decision makers or legal guardians in African American families compared with Caucasian families? What are the special and unique considerations practitioners must consider in this case, if any?

Meeting Mrs. Smith's Daughter

When she arrived later that day, I spoke with Tammy, Mrs. Smith's daughter. Tammy confirmed that she was Mrs. Smith's only child. She also confirmed the niece's account about problems between extended families and their subsequent decision to care for their respective parents. Tammy claimed that neither family was happy that the couple married so late in life (both were in their mid-seventies), and that many of the problems between the families revolved around money, inheritance, and end-of-life care. However, they had made no firm decisions about these issues.

Sure that her mother would recover, Tammy intended for her to return to the nursing home once she was medically stable. Tammy did not mention the possibility that her mother would die, and I decided not to bring it up at this time. She also said that she was unaware of any end-of-life planning her mother and stepfather prepared. In fact, she was sure they did not have a plan. I asked Tammy to serve as her mother's surrogate decision maker. She agreed and signed the appropriate paperwork. At my request, she agreed to keep her stepfather and his family informed about Mrs. Smith's current medical plan. I did not want Mr. Smith's family to step in without warning. By asking her to communicate with them, I was trying to ensure that they would participate in the decision-making process.

When a family member's health takes a turn for the worse, rendering them incapacitated and/or incompetent, the rest of the family experiences periods of uncertainty and there are certain to be differing opinions about what should happen or about their loved one's "wishes." Few families prepare in advance for these issues, so they routinely are caught off guard when it occurs. Hence, healthcare institutions and physicians treating an unconscious or incompetent adult cannot always rely on a consent form signed by a spouse or relative since everyone tends to have their own opinions about the required course of action. Although, obtaining consent often strengthens the doctor-patient relationship and in some circumstances, provides a measure of legal protection.

Because Mrs. Smith's family (Tammy) agreed that she should return to her nursing home when her condition stabilized and she was her only relative, we considered Tammy an appropriate surrogate decision maker for Mrs. Smith's current situation. Yet, this was not a legally binding arrangement, so I was uncertain about how much power she actually had in final decision making. It might only become an issue if Mrs. Smith's condition became imminently life threatening.

Unfortunately, early on in the process problems emerged regarding Tammy as decision maker. This pattern served as a warning for the future. She rarely visited the hospital. I tried contacting her at home to offer emotional support. Tammy usually reported that she was feeling fine. However, occasionally Tammy expressed feeling overwhelmed with the added responsibility of her mother's care. Her infrequent visits and feelings of being overwhelmed are common for family members during times of crisis or change. Tammy was preoccupied with stress in her personal life in addition to the stress involving her mother's condition. Medical crises never seem to occur when people have the time to handle them. As Tammy stated, "I have my mother to worry about . . . and my own life. Life does go on."

Tammy told me that she had not seen her mother much in recent years. They had drifted apart when Mrs. Smith met and married Mr. Smith. Tammy did not like his extended family. She thought that they tried to control the Smiths and was worried that they (Mr. Smith's family) were only interested in whatever money he and her mother might have. Therefore, Tammy and her mother had fallen out of touch. Certainly, she had no idea what her mother wanted for herself when and if this type of situation occurred.

There was another complicating factor for Tammy. She had also been the primary care provider and decision maker for two other family members who eventually died. She confessed that she was not ready to go through another significant loss. This experience played a significant role in problems we had later regarding Mrs. Smith's care.

In addition to her mother, Tammy also had two adult daughters living in her home along with one grandchild. She was a busy person. In an effort to gain control of her situation, Tammy tried to involve her two daughters in the decision making for Mrs. Smith. Tammy wanted to avoid becoming isolated during this difficult time. She needed support. I encouraged Tammy to find a social support network of friends and family to help support her through this period. I also supported her desire to involve her daughters in Mrs. Smith's care and decision making.

Questions

Now that the author has presented more information about Tammy and the Smith family, perform the following exercises based on your education, experience, the professional literature, and the available best practice evidence. To increase your learning potential, you may want to do this in a small group with other students in your course. Granted, there is not a lot of information to go on, compared with the amount of client information usually obtained in a clinical assessment. However, this is the information provided in this particular case, and as the responsible social worker, you must act.

1. **Based on the information shared, construct a three-generation genogram and eco-map that represent Mrs. Smith's personal, familial, and environmental circumstances. What further information do you need to complete this exercise? What patterns do these two important graphical assessment tools demonstrate?**

2. **Make a list of the issues and strengths in this family, drawing from multi-systemic sources.**

3. **Write a two- to three-page narrative assessment that encompasses Mrs. Smith's multi-systemic issues and strengths. Review Chapter 1 if needed. This narrative should provide a comprehensive and multi-systemic explanation of their life as they prepare to deal with their critically ill mother.**

4. **Try to identify the theoretical model or approach that you use to guide your assessment. According to the literature, what other theoretical options are available and how would these change the nature of your assessment?**

Difficult Decisions

Within days of our meeting, Mrs. Smith's healthcare team called a family meeting to share their prognosis and recommendations. The news was not good. The doctors did not believe that Mrs. Smith would ever successfully wean from life support. They had tried to wean her from the ventilator several times, and each attempt failed. She no longer had the capacity to breathe unassisted. Without a ventilator, Mrs. Smith would surely die. Tammy and her daughters took this news badly. They were unprepared for this eventuality. At that moment, I wished that I had mentioned this possibility earlier. Perhaps I could have prepared her for this moment. While she did not want her mother to suffer, she also did not want to be the one to "pull the plug" on her life.

The healthcare team explained Mrs. Smith's current condition and her options. The physician offered Tammy the option of removing Mrs. Smith from life support and allowing "nature to take it course." This phrase is commonly used to help patients and families understand that removal of life support does not mean that they are "killing" their loved one. In these cases, allowing nature to take its course means that they have the option of allowing her to live or die based on her ability to breathe naturally. This often relieves family members of any guilt for refusing aggressive medical intervention. It did not work for Tammy.

The physician was clear that he thought Tammy should accept this option, since Mrs. Smith would die without mechanical support of the breathing machine and she had no hope for any quality of life. The alternative plan offered to the family was to transfer Mrs. Smith to a ventilator dependent unit in a different facility where a medical team could continue the weaning process. Either way, the doctor made it clear that Mrs. Smith no longer required intensive care in an acute care setting such as our hospital and had to move, soon.

After a long and tearful discussion, Tammy and her daughters appeared ready to remove Mrs. Smith from life support. However, Mr. Smith was not ready to take this step. His family supported his decision to keep his wife alive at all costs. While Tammy was the sole decision maker, because of the complex family dynamics and the life-and-death decision the family faced, the process became a stalemate. Ultimately, Tammy backed off her decision to end life support. The problem was that she ultimately made no decision.

Legal Guardianship

As time passed and because of the problems within the family, I determined that Mrs. Smith probably needed the court to appoint a legal guardian to help guide the family through this difficult decision. My supervisor supported this recommendation. I believed that the split between the extended families and her fear of additional losses rendered Tammy unable to make this difficult decision.

The courts prefer to appoint a family member as guardian whenever possible. However, judges will appoint a nonfamily member to this position when nobody in the family wants the responsibility, it does not appear that the family can work out a decision, and/or if the judge determines that family members would provide improper representation. In this case, I believed that the family would not be able to work out a decision regarding Mrs. Smith's future because of the long history of problems between extended families. Moreover, for this and other reasons, I did not believe that Tammy was the person to manage this difficult job alone.

While Tammy had been reasonable to this point, she was in a difficult position. Since she had expressed her fear about facing more loss and was under significant stress, she struggled in her role. When I spoke with the family about this, I explained that the judge would appoint a temporary legal guardian. I explained that this was a legal and binding decision that could be changed only by returning to court. They seemed open to this suggestion. In fact, Tammy seemed relieved. Many times, the suggestion of the need for a legal guardian causes resistance and hostility. That was not the case here, initially. I believed that everyone simply wanted someone else to make the decision. Both extended families agreed to pursue a legal, temporary guardian appointment through the court system.

However, the judge appointed Tammy as the temporary guardian. For a while after her appointment, the healthcare team could not reach her and she did not return my telephone calls. Once I did make contact, Tammy requested another family meeting. I suspected that she was having second thoughts about withdrawing life support. Tammy and the family, including Mr. Smith and his family members, met with the physician to discuss their options. I explained to the healthcare team and family that if Tammy decided to withdraw life support, the local hospice organization would support Mrs. Smith during the transition and help the family deal with the numerous issues surrounding death and dying. I further explained that if Tammy decided to keep Mrs. Smith on the ventilator, I could arrange a transfer to an appropriate facility. I had already located two ventilator-dependent units in the city with open beds.

After much thought and discussion, Tammy decided against withdrawing life support. Moreover, she wanted her mother to remain in the hospital. Tammy explained to the team that she was not ready to let her mother die and was adamantly opposed to moving her mother to another facility. While we provided her with options, this was not one of them. Having Mrs. Smith remain in our hospital was not an option. She no longer needed the level of service we provided. She had two choices: remove life support or have her mother transferred to an appropriate facility. She refused both options. When the team and I pushed her for a decision that was possible, she declined.

Over the next couple of days, Tammy and I talked numerous times about her decision and its impact on her mother's future. She was not prepared to budge, and I could not allow her decision to stand. Since we were in a decision-making mode, I operated from the cognitive model. According to Turner (1986),

> Our objective is to help people think about and plan appropriate solutions. In these situations, the focus is on responsibility, ability, and effective use of one's executive capacities to deal with the present and function better in the future. (p. 653)

I sympathized with Tammy, validated her struggle, and encouraged her to visit the ventilator units and decide on a plan for Mrs. Smith. She refused. Instead, Tammy stated that she and her family believed that her mother would recover, and that the hospital was the best place for her to accomplish that. In the heat of the moment, and under the stress of having to make a life-or-death decision about her mother, Tammy suggested an option that resulted in no decision.

At this point, the hospital began putting pressure on the healthcare team and me to reach a suitable conclusion to this case. Mrs. Smith was receiving a level of care that was inappropriate for her needs, stopping others in need from receiving appropriate care, and costing her insurance provider and the hospital a lot of money.

I believed that Tammy's denial of her mother's declining health and her guilt prevented her from making a decision on behalf of her mother in the role as temporary guardian. I worked hard with her, offering Tammy room to process her emotions and utilize her untapped strengths in an effort to help her make a decision about her mother's future. I also worked to help Tammy find a way to be at peace with whatever decision she eventually made about her mother. I tried to avoid pressuring her to decide, yet, according to the hospital, Tammy would have to make a decision soon. However, my approach did not work and Tammy essentially stopped talking to me.

Ethical Challenges

Many on the healthcare team struggled with Tammy's indecisiveness and became frustrated with her disappearances when they tried to contact her. Sometimes, team members are too quick to decide on treatment plans for patients and then struggle when the patient or family opts for alternative plans. Medical professionals are accustomed to working with critically ill patients. They have a clear understanding of the medical condition and prognosis, and do not have the same emotional attachments as family members.

In my role as their social worker, I advocated for the Smith family and appreciated their struggle. I explained the various approaches to death that people have, and discussed with the healthcare team the power of denial as a defense mechanism. As professionals, we must respect how external factors influence decisions, and Tammy was a classic example of this. Working from the systems theory helped this become more evident.

One team member suggested that the Smith case go before the hospital Ethics Committee. This individual was frustrated that the family wanted to keep Mrs. Smith alive; they perceived this to be cruel and unnecessary in her current medical state. One team member was confused about the family's absences and interpreted this behavior as evidence of neglect, requiring a call to the local Adult Protective Services unit. This particular individual hoped that the Ethics Committee would change the outcome and force Tammy and the family to take action.

I explained that Tammy, as the legal guardian, had the right to keep her mother on life support. Tammy was doing what she thought her mother would want for herself. Hence, involving the Ethics Committee would not change the outcome. To clarify, when Tammy's struggles with the guardianship responsibilities became apparent, contacting the courts to review her appropriateness in the guardianship role was a more advisable step than consulting the Ethics Committee. The courts generally lean toward preserving life. My supervisor agreed with this position rather than involving the Ethics Committee.

The Importance of Supervision

This is a good time to discuss the importance of good supervision with difficult and confusing cases. Access to supervision in the hospital setting is helpful. With the complexity of the cases we manage on a daily basis, it is reassuring to speak with a supervisor about the legal aspects of a case, to have the opportunity to debrief, and to explore alternative perspectives. Supervision was an important factor during Mrs. Smith's case for all of these reasons.

Supervision is also the time for social workers to evaluate their levels of stress. It is important to have support systems in place in and outside of work. It is not enough to press through your day to get to your yoga class or the gym to de-stress. Having opportunities to de-stress at work helps to refocus and reenergize you so that you can continue through the day with focus and drive. For example, some social workers may take a walk during lunch, while others go to their supervisor for guidance. Various other health promotion and stress relief techniques are encouraged as well.

My supervisor helped me to remember that Tammy was acting appropriately as a daughter. As my supervisor stated, because Tammy did not cooperate with the hospital and refused to make a disposition decision, I had to act on behalf of the hospital. The hospital provides a service to the community. When resources are spent on an individual who does not need an acute level of care, my job is to discharge patients to a more appropriate level of care. This allows the hospital to admit someone from the community who needs intensive care services, since the beds are limited. In this instance, I indirectly worked for the good of the community, by insisting that Mrs. Smith move to an appropriate level of care outside intensive care.

A key topic of discussion in supervision about the Smith case was my struggle over replacing Tammy as temporary guardian. As we discussed earlier, a hospital social worker functions in multiple roles. With the Smith case, I operated primarily at the micro level, serving the patient and family, and from the mezzo-level, serving the healthcare system. I recognized Tammy's attempts to be involved and wanted Tammy to be successful at representing her mother.

I tried to advocate for Tammy, knowing that she struggled with her mother being critically ill. I also wanted her to feel a sense of control. Unfortunately, Mrs. Smith's situation demanded a quicker response than Tammy was able to provide. It became difficult for me to work with Tammy through this struggle because she closed herself off and refused further help. Tammy also closed off communication with other healthcare team members. This left me no alternative but to petition the courts for a new temporary guardian for Mrs. Smith.

Questions

In the previous pages, the author presented several issues for discussion, including ethical challenges and the need to move Mrs. Smith for the good of the larger community. She also mentioned the pressure brought to bear by the hospital over resources and money.

1. List the various issues that have ethical, legal, or financial implications.

2. Explore the practice literature and the code of ethics to address the issues mentioned above. According to your findings, analyze the author's approach and explain your position on each by using the literature, your experience, and the input of classmates obtained through dialogue.

3. How would you have handled these issues if you were the social worker responsible for this case? Explain and defend your positions.

Appointing a New Guardian

On behalf of the hospital and family, I was responsible to keep the court informed about the progress or problems with temporary guardians. This is especially true when temporary guardians struggle with their obligations. By doing this, I help judges make informed decisions at a second hearing about whether the existing temporary guardian was working out. The judge also recognized Tammy's struggle. Consequently, the judge assigned a new court-appointed temporary guardian for Mrs. Smith.

When he assumed his new role, Tim, the guardian made it clear to the health-care team that he would not request withdrawal of life support unless everyone in the family agreed. This was expected. Outside temporary guardians rarely decide to withdraw life support unless the family agreed. That decision was too big to make without family support.

The new guardian immediately requested a family meeting. He also asked a representative from one of the local ventilator-dependent units to attend. In this meeting were the extended families, Mrs. Smith's physician, the nurse, and myself. We reviewed Mrs. Smith's situation. After approximately two hours, the family agreed to remove Mrs. Smith from life support. However, they wanted to make this move after a few days, allowing the family time to visit Mrs. Smith and say their goodbyes. While this was a difficult decision, when it came everyone agreed it was the correct decision to make on behalf of Mrs. Smith, given the seriousness of her condition and her age.

During the weekend, Mrs. Smith's fever (one of many she had experienced since her admission) went down. Despite the physician's opinion of Mrs. Smith's overall prognosis, the family interpreted this as a sign that she was about to recover. Tammy called Tim and the doctors, forbidding them from removing Mrs. Smith from the ventilator. They wanted so badly to believe that Mrs. Smith would make a miraculous recovery and did not want to live with the guilt of having ended all possibility that a miracle could occur. We were back to "square one" with this case.

Consequently, Tim gave the hospital legal permission to transfer Mrs. Smith to a ventilator-dependent unit. He recognized the family's struggle and supported their desire to keep Mrs. Smith on life support. He was also aware that it was inappropriate to keep someone in Mrs. Smith's condition in the intensive care unit. Hence, he gave the hospital written permission, with the family's blessing, to transfer Mrs. Smith immediately.

Termination

The hospital transferred Mrs. Smith to a ventilator-dependent unit the next day. Since my relationship with Tammy soured over our disagreements about legal guardianship, I did not have the chance to close with her. I also did not have an opportunity to meet with any other family members. Termination in hospital social work is generally quick. When someone discharges from the hospital, the relationship generally ends. In this case, my relationship with Tammy ended long before we transferred Mrs. Smith out of the hospital.

Once the court appoints a legal guardian, we must work through the guardian for all treatment decisions. In this case, once Tim was appointed, Tammy no longer chose to interact with the healthcare team or me. While my decisions angered the family, I believe to this day that they were correct and in the best interest of everyone involved, including the Smith family and the hospital.

Conclusion

The Smith case offered a unique look at how I had to adapt how I interacted with patients and families with changing situations. I used several methods, depending on the situation.

Hospital social workers are instrumental during times of crisis. They help patients access the services they need with an understanding of what their insurance will cover. When patients without support cannot help themselves, they can rely on social workers to help. They become their advocate and work along side them to reach their goals.

Hospital social work is a rewarding and exciting field of practice. It presents many challenges and opportunities to help make a difference in people's lives. Applying the principles of social work theory and practice to everyday hospital situations is an effective means to assist patients and families coping with life-altering situations.

Questions

The author presented an interesting case that involved several multi-systemic issues. Taking a broad view of this case, reevaluate the author's work and your participation through the questions asked throughout the case.

1. Take a moment to review the case. Based on the author's description, the professional literature, and the latest practice evidence, what occurred to account for the outcome?

2. What was the theoretical approach or combination of approaches that appeared to work best for the Smith family?

3. Based on the work you have done earlier, what additional intervention(s) would you recommend? Use the literature and latest evidence to justify your recommendations.

4. Overall, what is your professional opinion of the work performed in this case? As always, refer to the professional literature, practice evidence, your experience, and the experience of classmates when developing your opinion.

5. Based on this review, what additional or alternative approaches would apply with this case? That is, if you were the practitioner, how would you have approached this case? Please explain and justify your approach.

6. What did this case demonstrate that you could use in other practice settings. List the most important things you learned by studying this case and how you could use them in your practice career.

7. Review the various systems that the author encountered and considered in this case and comment on how the author handled this aspect and what changes you would make if you were responsible for the case.

Bibliography _____

Aiken, L. R. (1991). *Dying, death, and bereavement* (2nd ed.). Boston: Allyn and Bacon.

Johnson, J. L. (2004). *Fundamentals of substance abuse practice.* Pacific Grove, CA: Brooks/Cole.

National Association of Social Workers (2000). *Code of Ethics of the National Association of Social Workers.* Washington, DC: Author.

Showalter, J. S. (1999). *The law of healthcare administration* (3rd ed.). Chicago: Health Administration Press.

Turner, F. J. (1986). *Social work treatment: Interlocking theoretical approaches* (3rd ed.). New York: The Free Press.